The Way We Were

THE OPEN SKIES

The Way We Were

THE OPEN SKIES

Wayne L. Youngblood

United Air Lines

UNITED

STATE OF
CALIFORNIA

CHARTWELL
BOOKS, INC.

This edition published by:

CHARTWELL BOOKS, INC.
A Division of
BOOK SALES, INC.
114 Northfield Avenue
Edison, New Jersey 08837

ISBN 13: 978-0-7858-2442-8
ISBN 10: 0-7858-2442-1

© 2008 by Compendium Publishing Ltd.
43 Frith Street, London W1D 4SA,
United Kingdom

Cataloging-in-publication data is available from the Library of
Congress.

Designer: Dave Ball
Color reproduction: Anorax
Printed in: China

Page 1:
Flying Aces **magazine, March 1936**
As flight fever grew, so did
publications to help hobbyists' enjoyment. *Flying
Aces* magazine served to meet the needs of those
seeking aerial "fiction, model building, and fact."
Photo courtesy of the author

PAGES 2-3:
DC-3, United Airlines, 1939
An early picture of NC16072 *State of California.*
The National Archives

THIS PAGE:
**THE *Hindenburg*, LAKEHURST, NEW
JERSEY, 1930S**
Although the crash of the *Hindenburg* was not the
greatest loss of life on a rigid airship it did attract
the most attention and effectively ended the reign
of the airship. *The National Archives*

CONTENTS

LEFT:
THE AIR SHIP, 1898
Near the beginning of the 20th century many felt that in the near future most everyone would have personal airship devices. This musical farce poster exaggerates, but captures the feeling. *The Library of Congress Prints & Photographs Division*

ABOVE:
CROPDUSTING, 1942
Many wartime aircraft found secondary lives as low-flying rural farm cropdusters, spraying chemicals to control pests. Seabrook Farm, Bridgeton, New Jersey, John Collier photographer. *The Library of Congress Prints & Photographs Division*

INTRODUCTION

As you fly over the countryside in a modern jet-powered aircraft covering hundreds of miles per hour, it is easy to forget that our ability to benefit from powered flight is just barely over a century old. But the relative newness of powered flight in the role of human existence is not a result of a lack of desire or the want of trying. History is littered with the debris of failed attempts at human flight. It wasn't until the first successful takeoff by Orville and Wilbur Wright in 1903 that the right combination of technology, opportunity, and sweat came together to achieve successful powered heavier-than-air flight. It's been an incredible ride since, with the development of the biplane, monoplane, twin-engine, turbo-prop, helicopter, and various jets, to name just a few, and then spacecraft, which broke the bounds of gravity altogether. The industry of commercial flight has expanded along with the numerous technological advances of the 20th century, changing and developing to meet the needs of the day, whether new navigational tools, higher-speed engines, or special silverware for in-flight dining.

One of the things my wife brought to our marriage years ago was a very sturdy steel spoon engraved "IOWA," which she had found at some thrift shop along the way. It was a piece of flatware that had been designed for—and used by—Air Iowa, one of the dozens, if not hundreds, of

"The future doesn't belong to the faint-hearted. It belongs to the brave"

RONALD REAGAN, **January 28, 1986**

tiny commercial airlines that sprouted, blossomed, and ultimately withered, during the middle to later part of the 20th century.

This token reminder of days past, one of the few remaining artifacts from this now-defunct airline, is just a tiny representative of the countless dreams, memories, and journeys lived by those who were finally able to overcome gravity and fly like a bird (almost) with the successful introduction and development of the airplane and commercial aviation. To them, it wasn't a matter of if we'd learn to fly, it was when. It's perhaps more than a little ironic that viable air travel came hard on the heels of successful automobiles (both really made possible by the internal combustion engine), and that their development as tools of transportation ran parallel during much of the 20th century. It's kind of like learning to walk and run simultaneously. Both served to lift the curse of distance and time, making most areas of our own vast country readily available, and the opportunity of visiting other

countries possible for many who would otherwise experience little of the world

The IOWA spoon also serves as a reminder of the many past amenities of "the friendly skies" that helped make countless travelers more comfortable with the concept of flying. Many of these amenities have been lost one by one during the past several decades due to increased investor demand for corporate profits, as well as the need to address various security issues. The little luxuries offered by the airlines included flatware, china, and fancy napkins, as well as champagne breakfasts, gourmet food, playing cards, personalized service and, occasionally, even entertainment. But this wasn't the case in the beginning.

Virtually everything about early commercial air was male territory. Pilots were expected to fly the plane and take care of the mail (and, later, freight). Those few passengers who might be aboard were essentially expected to fend for themselves. As the airlines and their cargo grew, more men were added to flight crews (aerial couriers, airplane attendants, cabin boys, flight attendants or stewards, as they were known). Such additions were, however, inconsistent at best. These young men primarily loaded baggage and ticketed passengers, although they did sometimes offer inflight services such as passing out chewing gum (for ears) and occasional snacks.

In 1930, a young woman named Ellen Church approached Steve Stimpson of Boeing for a job. Church was a registered nurse, who also had taken flight lessons. Although she initially wanted to be a pilot, Church and Stimpson set up the first stewardess jobs and, on May 15, 1930, eight nurse-stewardesses became part of an experimental three-month program. Church was on the first such flight (Oakland to Chicago).

Initially, pilots weren't in favor of stewardesses, claiming they didn't have time to look after "helpless females," and it is reported that some pilots' wives started a letter-writing campaign to get rid of stewardesses. But this soon passed, as these young women proved their worth. One thing that did persist for a number of years, however, was the so-called "no marriage" rule. Until well into the 1960s, most airlines forbade stewardesses to marry. United Airlines kept the rule as a condition of employment until November 7, 1968.

According to Stimpson, in a speech he gave on the 25th anniversary of stewardess service, there was a good reason for the no-marriage rule: "As to married stewardesses," Stimson said, "we hired only one—that we know of—and that was very early and when we were in a great hurry. Miss [Ellis] Crawford would be out on a trip and be delayed by bad weather and/or other causes, sometimes for several days, and her husband would phone me around 3 o'clock in the morning and say, 'Mister, where is my wife?' "

The stewardess experiment was a complete success, and Church, who became chief stewardess, was deluged

with applicants. "The friendly skies" were off to a running start.

The idea of becoming a stewardess soon became nearly as glamorous for young rural girls as becoming a movie star. A number of stewardess schools soon sprang up and at least one—McConnell Schools (which operated in New York, Chicago, Minneapolis, Kansas City and Los Angeles)—made a business of recruiting young women to become "Starlets of the Skyways." A promotional mailing received by my mother in 1948 offered "a fascinating career" in only eight weeks. Requirements included being between 5ft and 5ft 8in tall, between 100lb and 135lb in weight, single, "even" teeth (for a great smile), and a pleasing personality. If hired, a new stewardess could expect to earn between $150 and $180 per month.

For much of the middle of the 20th century air travel was a privilege, and those passengers who were able to fly were treated as guests—sometimes as royal guests. Airlines now vied for the reputation of having the best service, friendliest stewardesses or the tastiest food. Some even designed spacious cabins in which passengers could relax—even on small aircraft. Then, as air travel became more affordable to the masses and was utilized more extensively by business people, the focus on comfort decreased, and it became more about how to move as many people as profitably as possible. A recent airline advertisement even made a point of emphasizing the extra 6in of leg room it offered to passengers. However, even if you have to eat on your knees in a cramped seat, it's with the knowledge that it's flight nonetheless: something that was only a dream and nothing more for countless generations of people.

By physique we're a grounded, slow-moving species, but we've always remained jealous of the birds that are able to dip, swoop, and ride the thermals. Over the centuries

LEFT:
SKYSCRAPERS & PLANES, C. 1924
This pen and ink drawing by Frederick Coffay Yohn features a city scene clogged with aircraft of all types, a vision held by many as aircraft became a common vision in the sky. *The Library of Congress Prints & Photographs Division.*

ABOVE:
AUTOGIRO, 1938
Autogiros combine elements of both airplanes and helicopters. These airworthy craft met with little commercial success, mainly shuttling mail between Philadelphia and Camden, New Jersey. *Photo courtesy of author.*

A Fascinating Career

Your career as an Airline Stewardess-Hostess of the world's airways is a career filled with opportunity, variety and the romance of travel! You are a representative in the ship loft, of the line for which you work.

• Exciting Travel

• Fascinating Experiences

• Meet Interesting People

• Excellent Salary

Getting ready to "go places" in the industry of the future, McConnell students enjoy every hour of interesting class studies.

Fill out the Record on the other side of this sheet COMPLETELY. Do it NOW! If you are qualified, we will send you our large new Catalogue.

If you wish a more personal contact, go to one of the following McConnell School offices:

Mr. David	30 Rockefeller Plaza, New York	COlumbus 5-3593
Mrs. Moffet	333 North Mich., Chicago	ANdover 2511
Miss Pappen	1030 Nicollet Avenue, Minneapolis	BRidgeport 4238
Miss Earnshaw	1103 East Armour, Kansas City, Mo.	JEFferson 1233
Mr. Holden	631½ So. West Moreland, Los Angeles	DRexel 7447

McCONNELL SCHOOLS, 1948
After the experimental period of stewardesses proved to be a major success, establishments such as the McConnell Schools popped up, offering training to become a "starlet of the Skyway." *Image courtesy of author.*

Go to your library and ask for the December 8, 1947, issue of Life Magazine. Read the amazing story on the McConnell Air Hostess-Stewardess Schools on pages 83 - 87. You will see actual classroom scenes showing students who by this time are flying the nation's skyways.

"The Finished Flight" . . . The Airline Hostess—intelligent, alert, professionally poised to serve a discriminating public.

You will study such interesting subjects as Stewardess duties, Responsibilities and Conduct . . . Flight Routine . . . Meal Service . . . Theory of Flight . . . Aircraft Familiarization . . . History of Air Transportation . . . Flight First Aid . . . Comportment and Self-Development . . . Figure . . . Posture . . . Makeup . . . Voice, and many others.

DON'T DELAY — FILL IN THE QUESTIONNAIRE ON THE REVERSE SIDE NOW — SEE IF YOU QUALIFY FOR AN EXCITING NEW CAREER!

---

many men tried unsuccessfully to fly by attaching wing-like appendages to their arms or by building contraptions designed to triumph over gravity. As a small child I thought that if I believed and concentrated just hard enough I, too, could take off. I was, of course, misguided, but I was far from being alone in my dreams.

My first trip in an airplane at age 18 (in a tiny Piper Cub) was about the closest thing I knew to heaven on earth. The feeling of flight was both terrifying and wonderful. The near-falling sensation of banking, and the sudden dips caused by the current were incredibly liberating for mind, body, and soul, and left me with a love for flying that has never faded. I still feel like a child when I know I get to "ride in an airplane" (the smaller the better). Again, I know I'm not alone in this feeling. When I travel now, usually on large jets, it's unfortunately easy to forget that sensation of being way above the surface of the earth and experiencing the miracle of flight. I might as well be riding a bus. But the idea lingers.

Many people have grown up without actually flying, but that doesn't mean that flight doesn't capture their fancy or let their imagination run wild. Just seeing or hearing a plane flying overhead was enough to make me wonder about who was on board or where it was headed. And who can forget those house-rattling sonic booms as jets began breaking the sound barrier. Earlier generations were very much in awe of those who traveled by air.

One early stewardess of the 1930s, Inez Keller, found herself in a plane that ran out of gas and landed in a wheat field near Cherokee, Wyoming. "People . . . came in wagons and on horseback to see the plane," she started, "they'd never seen an aircraft before and they wanted to touch it and to touch me. One of them called me 'the angel from the sky.'" In areas where even the automobile was still uncommon the appearance of a plane was a true marvel. State and county fairs never failed to pack in crowds when airplanes or blimps were on hand.

The earliest successful ventures of flying began with a number of lighter-than-air experiments with balloons during the past few centuries, including successful balloon spying operations during the American Civil War. As the 19th century wound down and there was great optimism in the rapidly expanding technology built for the dawning of the 20th century, these flights and their successes led to fanciful depictions of the "airships to come," and the idea they would be the future's primary mode of transportation. These somewhat futuristic visions showed most everyone traveling in some sort of airship.

Eventually, lighter-than-air flight for commercial purposes centered around the rigid-frame, hydrogen-filled Zeppelins, which began carrying passengers regularly around 1910, four years before the first experimental passenger service of standard aircraft. The most well-known of these ships are the *Graf Zeppelin* and *Hindenburg*, sister ships that plied the skies during the 1930s. All passenger use of the Zeppelin was discontinued after the fiery crash of the *Hindenburg* in 1937.

The other stepchild of the commercial aviation industry is the helicopter; that is, aircraft that can lift off and land vertically. The idea of the helicopter dates back thousands of years to China, where children played with toys that did just that.

Centuries earlier, Leonardo da Vinci designed what he called an "aerial screw," which was a conceptual machine that relied on rotating blades to lift it.

The first helicopter as we know it, however, is the gyroplane. Invented in 1907, it needed 32 rotating blades to lift it 2ft off the ground. It would take another 30 years for a truly successful helicopter to be developed. Prior to the development of a successful helicopter, however, there

was the autogyro (or autogiro), which was almost a hybrid between an airplane and a helicopter. An autogyro has a fuselage similar to an airplane, but uses non-powered top rotating blades for lift (and relies on aerodynamic forces to turn them) instead of wings, but has an engine and a front propeller for thrust. Although autogyros were reasonably successful, they didn't inspire confidence, possibly because the blades were non-powered. The only real commercial application for autogyros in the United States was as carriers of airmail from Camden, New Jersey, to Philadelphia, Pennsylvania, during the late 1930s, lifting off and landing on rooftops.

The father of American helicopters was Igor Sikorsky (who emigrated from Russia). Sikorsky's VS-300, introduced in 1940, was, in fact, the first successful true helicopter. It used a large set of powered, rotating blades on its top (for lift), and a smaller set on the tail (for thrust and control). Although helicopters have never really been used widely as passenger aircraft, they have been vital for use with cargo, maneuvering in tight spaces and are ideally suited for medical and emergency services.

The largest focus of this book, however, is on standard fixed-wing aircraft, which is responsible for all but a tiny fraction of commercial aviation functions.

Although there were various experiments with manned heavier-than-air flight during the twilight years of the 19th century, it wasn't until Orville and Wilbur Wright made their first successful flights on December 17, 1903, at Kill Devil Hills, North Carolina, that people began to realize manned flight was a reality, and that it could be

SNAIL MAIL, 1921
By the early 1920s, when this image was created, many were beginning to recognize the potential of profitable airmail service to further the success of commercial flight. *Image courtesy of author.*

VIN-FIZ
THE IDEAL GRAPE DRINK

ABOVE:
VIN FIZ POSTCARD, 1911
Calbraith Perry Rodgers became the first pilot to successfully cross the United States by plane. Cards similar to this were sold along the way. *Image courtesy of Nutmeg Stamp Auctions.*

ABOVE RIGHT:
AERIAL MAIL, 1912
Even before the United States Post Office Department began official airmail service it did authorize flights at special events. Pilot Paul Studensky is shown receiving the mail for flight. *Image courtesy of Nutmeg Stamp Auctions.*

BELOW RIGHT:
FIRST FLIGHT, 1912
The first official airmail flight was marked by this special postcard in 1912. The plane, which flew 90m in 91min, crashed upon landing, preventing a scheduled return flight. *Image courtesy of Nutmeg Stamp Auctions.*

developed into a viable industry within a few years. By experimenting first with gliders, the Wrights were able to achieve sustained level flight and maneuverability—the two key things that make any kind of powered flight possible. Most inventors approached the problem as simply one of getting off the ground and ignored what came next (or didn't, as the case may be).

Another factor that undoubtedly helped the Wrights succeed, where many others had failed, was the deep and abiding respect they had for each other. They not only worked as a team but they were also able to critique each other's ideas honestly, arguing technical issues without hostility. They also served as objective and knowledgeable observers for each other's flight experiments, analyzing both the successes and failures competently.

By August 1908, when Wilbur Wright made the first successful public flight displays in Le Mans, France, there were still plenty of skeptics, most whom questioned whether the Wrights had been "liars or flyers," in regard to their earlier and rather secretive experiments. They were flyers.

Now that it was established that man could fly in one of these contraptions, the next step was to refine and find ways to carry passengers. This was accomplished successfully on New Year's Day 1914, when the Benoist Aircraft Co. (based in St. Louis) decided to provide a local air service between St. Petersburg and Tampa, Florida. The Benoist Type XIV flying boat took off from St. Petersburg with pilot Anthony Jannus and Mayor Pheil, bound for Tampa. The 22m journey took only 23 min (about 64mph) and proved that commercial flight was viable, if not necessarily profitable. The service was suspended in April of the same year because it wasn't making enough money.

A total of 1,205 passengers were carried during the three-plus months the Benoist service operated, and although there were 22 flight cancellations during that time, there wasn't a single major wreck or any fatalities. Passengers were charged $5 each (with a surcharge for those who weighed more than 200lb).

It took a few more years for commercial passenger aviation to truly take off, but when it did there were many in line who wanted to do it profitably. How liberating it must have been for those who had access to these early flights to be able to fly upwards of 70mph at a time when even the automobile was still far from the norm. Today we can eat breakfast in London, arrive in New York in time for lunch, and have supper in Los Angeles if we still have the energy.

Although there were several other passenger services that began fairly soon after the Benoist experiment, it wasn't until after World War I that commercial passenger flight became more viable and profitable on a larger scale. One of the things that made this possible was the use of converted World War I bombers, which could be used to carry both cargo and passengers (although not always comfortably). Freight was carried as early as 1910, when a bolt of fabric was flown from Dayton to Columbus, Ohio, beating the train. As with passenger services, however, freight flights weren't widely used until after World War I.

Spurred on by the Wrights' successes, many early pilots began taking to the air. Some carried passengers, some freight, others mail, and still others just wanted to fly. Whatever their reasons, many were convinced that commercial air travel would open up business and commerce like nothing had before. It was just a matter of opening up the sky . . .

The next few years brought a number of aerial tournaments, in which a number of different types of aircraft were tested in competition for the ability to fly, maneuverability, practicality, and speed. Some of these events were marked by unofficial mail carried by the pilots (with paid U.S. postage, of course). Today, these "pioneer flight covers," as they are called, not only mark these important events and the dates they were held but are also collected very avidly as well, some selling for thousands of dollars.

Among the early pilots who saw the future of aviation was a relatively young man by the name of Calbraith Perry Rodgers, who managed America's first trans-continental flight. Oddly, Rodgers, whose name should arguably be as well known as Lindbergh's for his accomplishment, is remembered almost exclusively for rare stamped postcards that bear the name of his sponsor.

Although Rodgers was among the first to study under the Wrights, he was an unknown when he stole the spotlight at the 1911 Chicago International Aviation Meet and won its $11,285 prize (more than a quarter of a million in today's currency). Rodgers, a descendant of military greats Captain Oliver Hazard Perry (of the Battle of Lake Erie), Commodore Matthew Perry (who was responsible for opening Japan to the world in 1854), and Rear Admiral Christopher Raymond Perry Rodgers (Union Navy during the Civil War), could not pursue a military career: he was nearly deaf. However, he did love speed.

Things were heating up quickly in the field of aviation. In October 1910, William Randolph Hearst announced a $50,000 award to be given to any pilot who could fly cross-country in fewer than 30 days and complete the journey by October 10, 1911. This was no small feat, since the distance between New York City and Los Angeles is greater than that between London, England and Cairo, Egypt!

By the time Rodgers won his money in Chicago, time was already running out for Hearst's challenge. Nonetheless, he thought he could win the competition and hurried to enter.

By mid-September, Rodgers had purchased two brand-new Wright flyers (one that cost $5,000) and lined up a sponsor—the Armour Meat Packing Co. of Chicago, Illinois. Armour was anxious to promote its new grape soft drink, called Vin Fiz, and apparently saw a great opportunity with Rodgers. In exchange for displaying the name and logo of the new drink on all flat surfaces of his plane, Rodgers was to receive $5 for every mile flown east of the Mississippi River, $4 for every mile flown west of the river, and an expense-paid private train that would trail the pilot and carry his spare plane, his wife, reporters, and Armour Co. employees.

On September 17, 1911, Rodgers took off from Sheepshead Bay in Brooklyn, New York, in his Vin Fiz Flyer, bound for California. Due to a number of reasons (not least of them was surviving three crashes), Rodgers took 21 days to reach Chicago. He arrived on October 8, just two days shy of the Hearst offer expiring. Rodgers had now flown only 1,000 miles of his planned 4,000-mile journey.

With the Hearst prize now absolutely out of reach, Rodgers made the decision to complete his historic journey anyway (the Armour money probably didn't hurt, either). He announced to reporters, "I am bound for Los Angeles and the Pacific Ocean." It was no longer about the prize. He continued: "I'm going to do this whether I get $5,000 or 50c or nothing. I am going to cross this continent simply to be the first to cross in an aeroplane."

Although no one is certain, it was probably around this time that the idea for Vin Fiz mail came about. Special 25c labels were printed that pictured the flyer and bore the inscription, "Rodgers Aerial Post." Rodgers' wife, Mabel, served as "postmaster" for this unofficial and unauthorized service, and made the offer that postcards mailed to her, care of the Plaza Hotel in Chicago, would be stamped, specially marked and carried aboard at least one leg of the

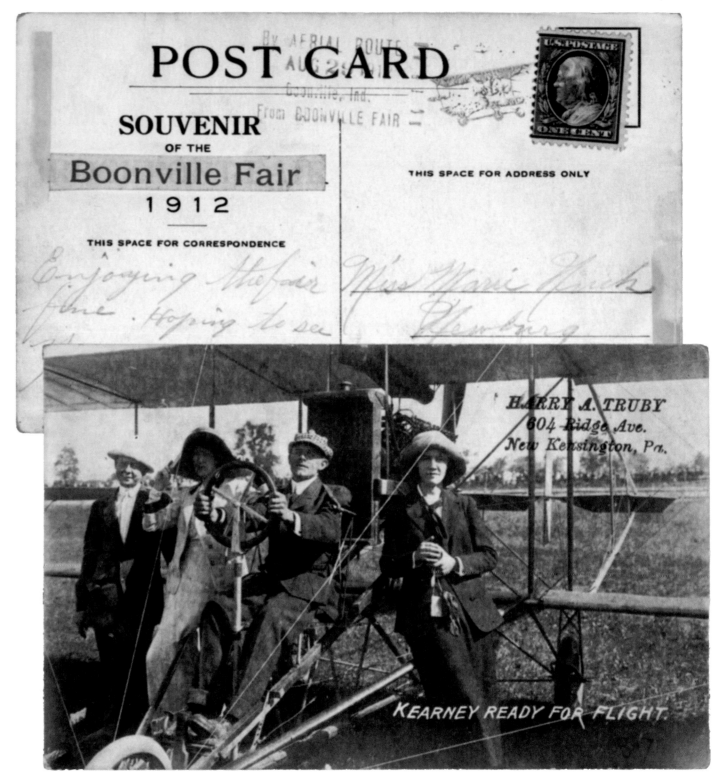

ABOVE:
AERIAL ROUTE, 1912
Fairs and air shows counted on aerial mail souvenirs to help pay the bills. Boonville, Indiana, even created a pictorial airplane cancel for mail flown 1m by pilot Horace Kearney. *Image courtesy of Nutmeg Stamp Auctions.*

ABOVE RIGHT:
VIN FIZ STAMP, 1911
A special (but unauthorized) stamp was created for Cal Rodgers transcontinental flight in 1911. It pictures Rodgers' Wright flyer and is extremely rare today. *Photo courtesy of author.*

RIGHT:
TAKEOFF, FORT RECOVERY, 1912
An early-model flyer is shown on this real-photo postcard taking off from the Harvest Festival Aviation Exhibition held in Fort Recovery, Ohio in 1912. *Image courtesy of Nutmeg Stamp Auctions.*

journey for the 25c fee (of course, full U.S. postage also had to be present). Stamps were also sold separately, as were picture postcards of Rodgers and his Vin Fiz Flyer. The earliest example is dated October 15, 1911, from Vinita, Okla.

Today, only a few stamped postcards have been found, and only four unused copies of the Vin Fiz stamp have turned up (the whereabouts of one is unknown). Stamped cards have a current retail of $50,000—the same amount as the original Hearst prize!

Rodgers took off from Chicago a few hours after he landed on October 8, finally landing in Tournament Park in Pasadena, California, on November 5. The journey had taken 49 days, spanned 4,321 miles at an average speed of 51.5mph, and Rodgers had survived 15 major accidents along the way. Even though he was close, Rodgers had not yet actually touched the ocean with his flyer, and he

thought it an appropriate thing to do.

On November 12, he took off from Tournament Park, headed for Long Beach—a journey that should only have taken a few minutes. Halfway to Long Beach Rodgers' flyer suffered a broken control wire, forcing him to make a terrible crash landing. He awoke in the hospital the following day with concussion, two broken legs, several cracked ribs, and he was also badly bruised and burned. But Rodgers was determined to finish, and stated that he'd do it in the same machine.

Almost a month later, after recovering from his wounds, Rodgers lifted off on December 10 from an alfalfa field near Compton, California., with his crutches strapped behind him in that "same machine" (likely only the rudder and engine drip pan remained). When he landed at Long Beach, 40,000 people were lined up to cheer him on. He taxied on the wet sand of the beach and aides pushed the wheels into the edge of the surf.

Slightly less than four months later, on April 3, 1912, Rodgers was flying over the same stretch of shoreline, when a flock of seagulls flew into his path, causing him to lose control. He died just yards from where he'd made his delayed—but highly triumphant—landing.

Rodgers' first crossing (and others later) proved that transcontinental air service was a realistic goal. It took only a few years for passenger, cargo and airmail services to graduate from a highly experimental venture to regularly offered services.

Although the U.S. Post Office Department didn't get the idea of airmail from Rodgers, his efforts no doubt contributed to a later, very active participation by the USPOD in the establishment of regular airmail service— a service that led directly to the profitability of most commercial flight. The first authorized U.S. mail carried by air was flown on September 15, 1911, by Earle L.

Ovington, who had worked as an engineering assistant to Thomas Edison. "As I had no baggage compartment," Ovington wrote, "I put the bag of mail on my lap." Official airmail service began on May 15, 1918, with an inaugural service between Washington, D.C., and New York City. A special airmail stamp, showing a Curtiss Jenny with #38262 (the number of the first plane to carry the mail) was released the same day. On that same day a collector discovered a sheet of 100 with an upside-down airplane, now known as the "Inverted Jenny" and arguably the most famous stamp ever issued.

The USPOD issued a number of specific rules for pilots, including the following:

• Don't take the machine into the air unless you are satisfied that it will fly.
• Never leave the ground with the motor leaking.
• Pilots should carry hankies in a handy position to wipe off goggles.
• If emergency occurs while flying, land as soon as you can.
• If you see another machine near you, get out of its way.

Contract airmail service soon followed and allowed operators to have a form of financial safety net. The fees charged for carrying airmail helped to underwrite the establishment and development of consistent passenger service.

Freight also helped pay the bills as passenger service grew slowly. During the late 1920s, several airlines began carrying freight regularly. In 1927, 45,859lb of freight was carried by air. In 1931, more than 1 million lb of freight were carried by air—representing more than a 2,000 per cent growth in just four years! Oddly, despite the success

of air freight, there were no all-cargo airlines until after the end of World War II, although United Airlines began operating some all-freight flights as early as 1940.

Throughout the 1920s to 1950s, passenger air service continued to evolve and grow, but this service received its greatest boosts after both world wars. This was due to several things, including the significant amount of technological development that was involved in creating wartime planes. Another significant boost was the large number of surplus planes that became available after the wars for conversion into peacetime passenger aircraft. These same boosts, ironically, also slowed some phases of development and production, since there was not the same level of demand for new aircraft after the wars ended.

Probably, one of the most important of any American aircraft was the highly reliable workhorse, the Douglas DC-3, introduced in 1936. The DC-3 was designed for American Airlines, with an initial anticipated total order of only 20. The 20-passenger accommodations of the DC-3 allowed it to stand alone from the necessary airmail contracts to make flight financially feasible. It also was able to fly cross-country, and nonstop between New York and Chicago, with only three fueling stops in about 15 hours. Offering sleeping berths helped as well to popularize air travel, and the plane was soon the most popular of all.

During World War II, military versions of DC-3s (including C-4s and C-53s) were important transport planes and many were converted at the war's end for passenger use. Although other manufacturers tried to update or surpass the design of this fixed-wing propeller-driven craft, it couldn't be replaced and was quite important to the aviation industry well into the 1970s. Despite the original anticipated need for only 20 DC-3s,

**NORTHWEST AIRLINES DC–3,
CA. 1936**
Passengers are shown boarding a
Northwest Airlines DC–3 at
Madison (Wisconsin) Municipal
Airport. The DC–3 is arguably the
most important aircraft created. *The
Wisconsin Historical Society
Historical Images.*

GOODYEAR BLIMP AT THE WISCONSIN STATE FAIR, C. 1936
The Goodyear Tire Company blimp hovers above the carnival area of the Wisconsin State Fair. Although fairgoers seem uninterested, airships captured the imagination of millions from the late 1800s through the 1930s. *The Wisconsin Historical Society Historical Images.*

more than 13,000 were eventually built, and more than 800 are estimated to still be in service!

The modern period of flight is punctuated by the start of the jet age, beginning with the invention of the first jet engine in 1930 by a British pilot, Frank Whittle, although it was not immediately developed further. Jets were not initially designed for commercial use. They were a byproduct of the burgeoning technology created for wartime use during the 1940s, as was the development of pressurized cabins, which not only stabilized oxygen levels, but the temperature as well, allowing aircraft to fly faster and at higher altitudes than older planes. The first such regular transatlantic service (with pressurized cabins) began with Pan American Airways on January 20, 1946.

Jets are designed to be far more powerful than any propeller plane could possibly be. Unlike a piston-driven propeller craft, a jet works on the principal that air is sucked in through turbofans and is compressed by traveling through spinning turbine blades. That compressed air is then expelled into a firing chamber, along with a spray of jet fuel. The resulting ignition and flame then expel the superheated and expanded gasses back through the exhaust nozzles, propelling the aircraft forward at great speed. Jet power also enabled aircraft to climb faster and fly at higher cruising altitudes. Despite these advantages, commercial aviation was slow to embrace the jet, mainly because of the expensive airport modifications.

In July 1949, the first jet airliner, the de Havilland Comet took off, and soon reached speeds well above anything a propeller plane could offer (a Comet reached 457mph in October 1949). Among other things, passengers were impressed by the fact that jets were much smoother and quieter than propeller planes. There were a couple of false starts, and some design

modifications were necessary to prevent metal fatigue at high speeds before the use of jets became widespread, but the die was cast. By the early 1960s most long-distance air travel was carried out by jets, although some of the larger and more efficient types of propeller planes continued to operate for years.

As mentioned previously, commercial aviation's focus eventually shifted from passenger comfort to moving as many people as possible as inexpensively as possible. The 1960s saw the rise of the jumbo jet—monsters of the skies that can carry hundreds of passengers.

By 1969, when the Boeing 747 Jumbo was introduced, passenger aircraft could carry more than 200 passengers. The 747 was so large that its first model was capable of carrying 400 people, in addition to having a lounge and other comfort areas. It has been noted that the wingspan of the original 747 is longer than the Wright Brothers' first flight! To construct the 747, Boeing had to build a larger plant at its home in Washington State. The Jumbo was too large to be assembled in any other facilities. Boeing Jumbos are still based on the 747 design, although they now can carry upwards of 500 passengers.

Additionally, a mention must also be made of the tiny private aircraft used by individuals all over the country. Cessnas, Pipers, Beechcraft and other small private craft are increasingly used—both for business and weekend hobby use—and flown by people who love flying in a very personal and "hands-on" way.

The images in this book cover three basic types of flight, including lighter-than-air, heavier-than-air, and helicopter, although no attempt has been made to be comprehensive in any of these vast and complex areas. The images chosen represent many different time periods, but all have a timeless feel about them.

THE EARLY YEARS AND PIONEERS

As the 20th century dawned and the internal combustion engine began offering more options than ever known for power, it occurred to bicycle-makers Orville and Wilbur Wright that heavier-than-air powered flight might be possible. Starting with gliders, the brothers worked on the aerodynamics first (to allow sustained, level flight) and then, in 1903, successfully flew the first powered aircraft at Kill Devil Hills, North Carolina.

The Wrights, who were secretive about their early flights, were not only fliers, however, but they were also photographers. They carefully documented many steps of their early flights. Despite an Ohio flood in 1913, which destroyed or damaged many of their records, a number of glass negatives and images of their early flights survive. Many others soon followed in their footsteps, designing all kinds of powered aircraft with varying levels of functionality. All, however, were interesting. Some were feasible, if not practical, while others were little more than flights of fancy.

"Air Fever" soon took over the entire nation, and—without exception—air shows, meets and other public displays of flight never failed to pack in the crowds.

LEFT:
POSTMISTRESS MRS. LATHROP,
c. 1919
Postmistress, "Mrs. Lathrop" (with helmet, leather jacket, and goggles) poses next to an airplane that was the first to land on Madeline Island, Wisconsin. *The Wisconsin Historical Society Historical Images*

RIGHT:
FIRST POWERED FLIGHT, DECEMBER 17, 1903, 10.35 A.M.
Orville Wright is shown making the historic flight (lying prone) while Wilbur runs alongside to balance the craft, which flew 120ft. *The Library of Congress Prints & Photographs Division*

PAULHAM'S AEROPLANE, C. 1910S
A crowd of people of all ages, complete with bicycles and an auto, surround this unusual craft awaiting its takeoff. Early aircraft never failed to attract attention. *The Library of Congress Prints & Photographs Division.*

EWS SERVICE

ABOVE:
HANRIOT MONOPLANE, C. 1910S
The Hanriot monoplane is one of many early craft of which little is known. It has an exaggerated long "stick" body, which has only limited practicality. *The Library of Congress Prints & Photographs Division.*

LEFT:
WRIGHT FLYER, 1910
A Wright racer prepares for takeoff at an early air meet in 1910. At right is an individual helping to maneuver the aircraft by hand. *The Library of Congress Prints & Photographs Division.*

PAGE 24:
STARTING AIRPLANE MOTOR, C. 1920S
To start many early larger aircraft it often took more than one man to crank the heavy, large propellers. The second man shown here is helping the first keep his balance. *The Library of Congress Prints & Photographs Division.*

PAGE 25:
FRANK COFFIN'S [SIC]
HYDRO-AEROPLANE, C. 1910S
Frank Coffyn (his name is frequently misspelled) designed an early hydroplane that he hoped would be used as a form of ferry/taxi in New York City, claiming the craft was safer than the taxicab. *The Library of Congress Prints & Photographs Division.*

STARTING AEROPLANE MOTOR

4848.9

LEFT:
AIRPLANE AND GROUP OF PEOPLE,
c. 1920s
Early air meets such as this were big events, and many people turned out in their Sunday finest to the fields in which they were held. *The Library of Congress Prints & Photographs Division.*

RIGHT:
AIRPLANE, c. 1920s
Early passenger service on aircraft such as this was fairly informal. Note the traveler's bags on the ground at his feet. *The Library of Congress Prints & Photographs Division.*

OVERLEAF:
WRIGHT GLIDER, 1911
Prior to motorizing their craft the Wrights worked with gliders to test aerodynamics. They continued to work with them as this 1911 example (resembling a normal flyer without engine) shows. *The Library of Congress Prints & Photographs Division.*

AIRMAIL ANNIVERSARY, 1919
Postmaster General Albert S.
Burleson (1913–21) was essential
to establishing a profitable airmail
service, celebrated on its first
anniversary in May 1919.
Milestones are noted on the banner.
*The Library of Congress Prints &
Photographs Division.*

WRIGHT'S START, SEPTEMBER 29, 1909
George Grantham Bain, an
important news photographer of the
early 20th century, snapped a
photographer photographing the
Wrights as they took off to fly over
New York Harbor in 1909. *The
Library of Congress Prints &
Photographs Division.*

WALTER CHRISTIE'S PLANE, 1910
Although J. Walter Christie is best
known for his military tank
suspension, he designed this plane
for the Belmont Park Meet, October
22–31, 1910. *The Library of
Congress Prints & Photographs
Division.*

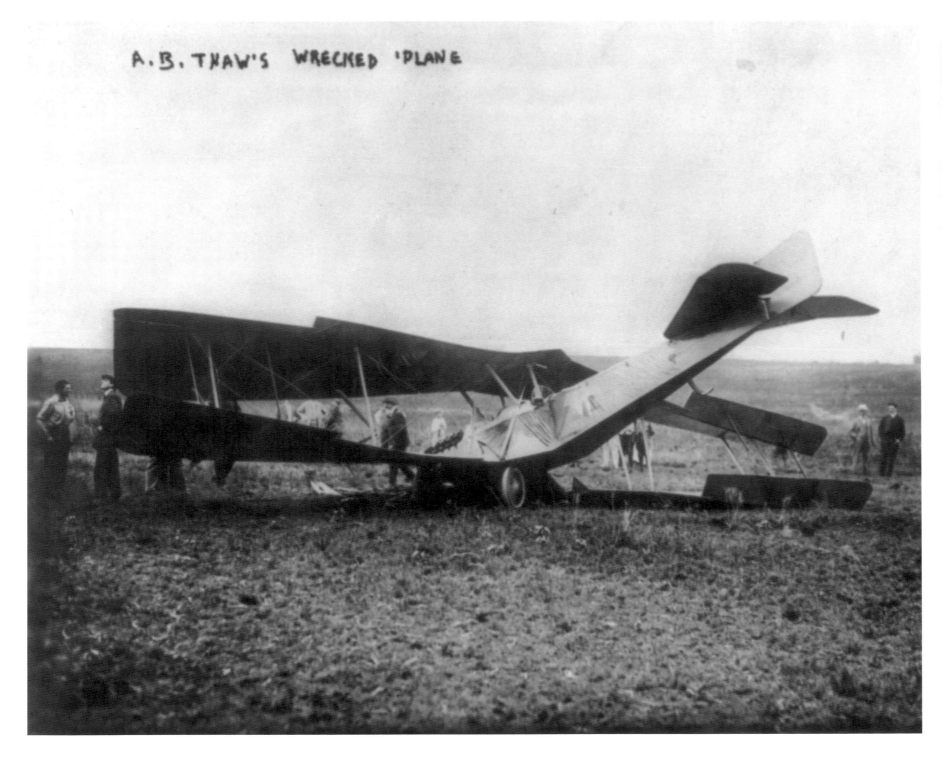

A.B. THAW'S WRECKED 'PLANE

ABOVE:
A.B. THAW, C. 1910S
A.B. Thaw, who starred in one movie in 1916 as an aviator (*My Country First*), had a mishap in an early airshow. The photo was simply captioned, "his wrecked plane." *The Library of Congress Prints & Photographs Division.*

RIGHT:
WRIGHT FLYER, 1911
Once the design of the Wright Flyer had been refined a little, carrying a passenger became possible, although not necessarily confidence-inspiring! *The Library of Congress Prints & Photographs Division.*

LEFT:

MISS E.L. TODD IN HER AIRPLANE, 1909

The world's first female airplane designer, E. Lillian Todd, sits in an aircraft of her design September 23, 1909. Although she also is attributed as the first woman to apply for a pilot's license she apparently flew only once. *The Library of Congress Prints & Photographs Division.*

TOP:

GLENN CURTISS IN HIS "JUNE BUG," JULY 4, 1908

Aviation pioneer Glenn H. Curtiss flies his "June Bug," aircraft, which won the Scientific American Trophy on July 4, 1908 at Hammondsport, New York. *The Library of Congress Prints & Photographs Division.*

ABOVE:

EARLY FLYING, C. 1910S

An early flyer, complete with steering wheel, flies over a small field in a city. Such flights usually managed to draw a crowd. *The Library of Congress Prints & Photographs Division.*

CAL RODGERS, 1911
Cal Rodgers (left), who made the historic first U.S. transcontinental flight in 1911 is shown getting out of his "Vin Fiz Flyer." *The Library of Congress Prints & Photographs Division.*

CURTISS MACHINE, 1910
A Curtiss machine, used by Glenn H. Curtiss in his flight from Albany, New York, to New York City, May 29, 1910. According to a note, the hydrosurface in the picture was removed and floats were substituted for the flight. *The Library of Congress Prints & Photographs Division.*

R.P. WARNER'S AEROPLANE IN FLIGHT, 1909
R.P. Warner's aeroplane, shown here in 1909, flying over a farming scene, emphasizes the contrast between early, complex contraptions and later, streamlined aircraft. *The Library of Congress Prints & Photographs Division.*

RIGHT:
HAMMOND AIRPLANE, 1911
The "Hammond," designed by Glenn Hammond Curtiss, is one of several of his machines. Curtiss is shown at the controls. *The Library of Congress Prints & Photographs Division.*

THE EVER-CHANGING AIRCRAFT

"Aeronautics was neither an industry nor a science. It was a miracle."

IGOR SIKORSKY

During the span of fewer than 50 years, powered aircraft evolved from a small plane that in 1903 traveled 120ft, to large Jumbo jets with wingspans longer than the duration of the Wrights' first flight. These modern-day monsters now cross oceans and vast land masses with ease that just a few generations ago were inaccessible via air.

Although there were major developments in aerodynamics and flight in every decade of the 20th century, the greatest visual changes in aircraft design arguably occurred during the early 1900s, when aircraft of all shapes and sizes began to appear. This was due in part to anticipated future uses (many of which never panned out) and refining the practicality of existing craft for uses that were developing, including freight and passenger service.

A great deal of the success in the development of aircraft during the first few decades is due to the fact that those who were designing them were working without the double-edged sword of experience, which can either further or muzzle creative development.

CIVIL AIR PATROL BASE, BAR HARBOR, MAINE, 1943
By utilizing civilian aircraft for semi-official duties during World War II, private aircraft were not completely grounded as they were in Britain. *The Library of Congress Prints & Photographs Division.*

NORTHWEST AIRWAYS MAIL DELIVERY, JULY 1, 1933
A Northwest Airways crew delivers a bag of airmail from a Ford TriMotor to Madison postmaster W.A. Devine. A passenger can be seen in the plane window. *The Wisconsin Historical Society Historical Images.*

ABOVE:
CLIPPER, C. 1930S.
A Clipper, a form of flying boat popular during the 1930s, is being towed ashore after landing. *Photo courtesy Bob Anderson.*

RIGHT:
NORTHWEST AIRLINES AIRPLANE, C. 1948
A Northwest Airlines passenger plane sits on the tarmac, being loaded and readied for takeoff. By the late 1940s air travel was becoming relatively common. *The Wisconsin Historical Society Historical Images.*

ABOVE:

MADISON AIRPORT AND TRAVELAIR, OCTOBER 23, 1930

A Travelair plane returns at night from a football game with photos for a newspaper. This photograph was made possible due to a beacon that safely guided pilots to the airport runway, a legacy of the U.S. Airmail Service. *The Wisconsin Historical Society Historical Images.*

NATIONAL AIR RACES, 1932
NR2101—a Granville Bros. R-1
Super Sportster, one of the most
exciting racing aircraft of the 1930s.
National Archives

NATIONAL AIR RACES, 1932
Short, stubby planes with low
wings, such as this Gee Bee R-1
racer, dubbed "The Flying Silo,"
allowed for maximum speed. *Photo
courtesy of Steve Turechek.*

THE UTICAN, 1938
Later racing planes, such as
Wendell Williams' 92 racer, had
slightly longer bodies than the Gee
Bee, but still featured low-placed
wings. *Photo courtesy of Steve
Turechek.*

LEFT:
FLAGG SPECIAL, 1937
The relatively small size of the
popular racers of the 1930s can be
seen in comparison to this United
Airlines DC-3. *Photo courtesy of
Steve Turechek.*

ABOVE:
LAWSON'S GREAT AIRLINER, 1921
The Lawson L-4 was designed and built by Alfred Lawson of Milwaukee to carry 34 passengers and 3 ton of mail, which was to be transferred through a chute to a small plane flying below to avoid landing. The L-4 crashed during its first test in 1921. This was likely an advance publicity photo. *The Wisconsin Historical Society Historical Images.*

RIGHT:
MOREY'S FLYING BILLBOARD, APRIL 17, 1928
Pilot Howard Morey not only flew, but advertised, and distributed Waco airplanes, and also operated a flying school. His diverse operations were typical of most commercial airline operations at the time. *The Wisconsin Historical Society Historical Images.*

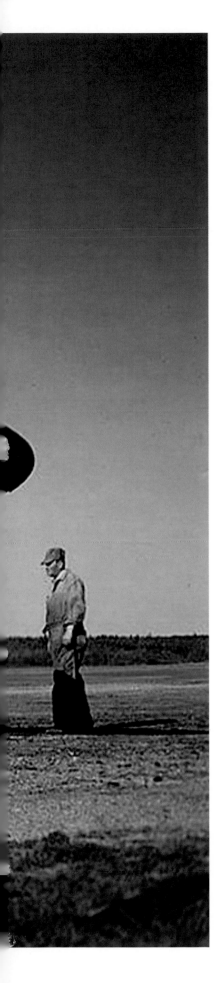

CIVIL AIR PATROL BASE, BAR HARBOR, MAINE, 1943
A number of private aircraft were used by the Civil Air Patrol (established in 1941) for border patrol and watch duties. *The Library of Congress Prints & Photographs Division.*

LEFT:
AV. CADET THANAS AT THE NAVAL AIR BASE, CORPUS CHRISTI, TEXAS, 1942
A cadet examines the propellers of his aircraft as part of a safety check before taking off from Corpus Christi, Texas, in 1942. *The Library of Congress Prints & Photographs Division.*

PLANE AT THE NAVAL AIR BASE, CORPUS CHRISTI, TEXAS, 1942
By the 1940s, virtually all but the very small private planes were large enough aircraft to be an imposing sight when confronted—quite a difference from early one- and two-seaters. *The Library of Congress Prints & Photographs Division.*

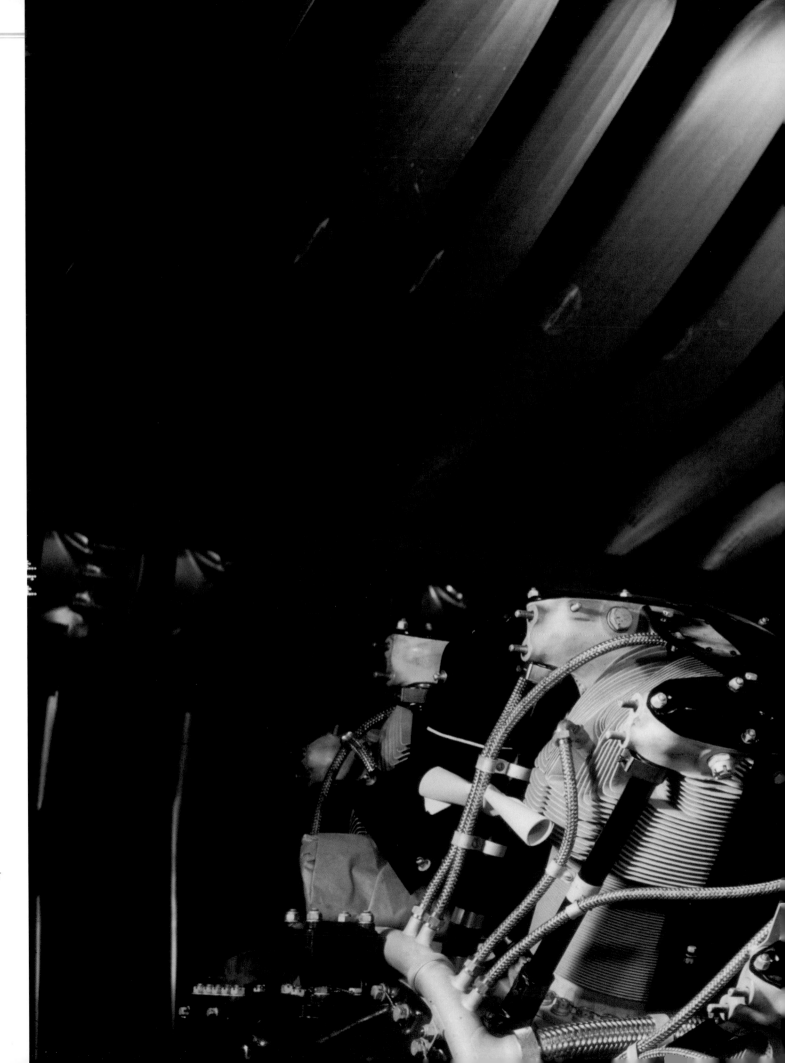

WOMAN WORKING ON AIRPLANE MOTOR, NORTH AMERICAN AVIATION, 1942
Between the increasing demand for commercial aircraft and the need for them during World War II, aircraft manufacturing became a leading field in the 1940s. *The Library of Congress Prints & Photographs Division* .

LEFT:

COWLING CONSTRUCTION, NORTH AMERICAN AVIATION, 1942

Because of the shortage of male workers during the war, many women, of all ages, went to work in aircraft manufacturing plants. *The Library of Congress Prints & Photographs Division.*

LEFT:

PAN-AM CLIPPER, 1935

A Pan-American Airways "Flying Boat" clipper sits moored at a dock in the Bahamas. The ability of flying boats to operate on water gained them much popularity. *The Library of Congress Prints & Photographs Division.*

ABOVE:

PEANUT ONE, 1976

As the jet age matured, presidents had their own Air Force One jets. President Jimmy Carter, a retired peanut farmer, christened his jet *Peanut One. The Library of Congress Prints & Photographs Division.*

RIGHT:
MARINE ONE, 1977
In addition to jet transport, presidents since Dwight D. Eisenhower have been transported on helicopters such as this, dubbed "Marine One." *The Library of Congress Prints & Photographs Division.*

BELOW:
THE PATRICIAN, 1929
The Patrician, dubbed as the "largest passenger plane yet to be produced," made its first flight in 1929 with 20 passengers and their luggage. *The Library of Congress Prints & Photographs Division.*

LEFT:
DISTRICT OF COLUMBIA, 1940
An American Airlines DC-3 named *District of Columbia* makes its first commercial flight to the newly opened Washington National Airport, September 28, 1940. *The National Archives.*

BELOW:
SIKORSKY S42 FLYING BOAT, 1934
A Sikorsky S42 flying boat operated by Pan American Airlines skims along the surface of the water on the Miami–Rio de Janiero route. *The National Archives.*

RIGHT:

WESTERN AIR EXPRESS, 1928
A Fokker F-10 trimotor, operated by Western Air Express service, is towed on the ramp at the Oakland Airport in 1928. *The National Archives.*

RIGHT:

CESSNA BOBCAT, ALASKA, CA. 1950
A Cessna Bobcat delivers mail in Alaska. A sled and husky team, as well as a sturdy truck, is ready to carry deliveries to outlying homes. *The National Archives.*

ABOVE:
CHICAGO MUNICIPAL AIRPORT, C. 1933
Two Ford Tri-motors sit in front of the Chicago Municipal Airport, awaiting taxi and takeoff in May 1933. The tri-motor became a popular aerial workhorse. *The National Archives.*

LEFT:
LOADING WINE, SPRINGFIELD, OHIO, c. 1930s
Loading wine for shipment by air, perhaps to Rattlesnake Island, an isolated island in Lake Erie that early on relied on air transport. The tri-motor became a popular aerial workhorse. *The National Archives.*

AIRSHIPS

Airships (also known as dirigibles, Zeppelins, blimps, and lighter-than-aircraft), those enormous cigar-shaped behemoths of the sky, were actually an outgrowth of hot-air balloons. The largest of these, sister ships *Graf Zeppelin* and *Hindenburg*, were each more than 800ft long (longer than three modern jumbo jets parked end-to-end). Most were either of semi-rigid or rigid construction. French engineer Henri Giffard created the first controlled dirigible in 1852, when he filled his balloon with hydrogen and attached a three-horse-power steam engine and a rudder to make a controlled flight from Paris to Trappes (about 17m). His steam engine was replaced in 1872 with an internal combustion engine created by Paul Haenlein. This also was the first time an internal combustion engine had been used in any experiments with flight. By the early years of the 20th century (around 1910), German airships were already carrying passengers regularly. They were extremely popular until the *Hindenburg* disaster of 1937, when the hydrogen caught fire as the airship was docking in Lakehurst, New Jersey, burning out in less than a minute.

As an interesting side note, the spire of the Empire State Building (completed in 1931) was designed to be a mooring post for airships, but was never used.

Although the airship is most closely associated with the Germans, the United States Navy also operated several, including the *Shenandoah*, *Macon*, *Akron*, and *Los Angeles* (all part of World War I reparations from Germany), and the U.S. Navy used a number of non-rigid blimps during the 1940s.

ABOVE:
Marine Corps air station, Tustin, California undated
The massive airship hangars were converted for other uses after airships were abandoned. This hangar served as a Marine air station. *The Library of Congress Prints & Photographs Division.*

ABOVE RIGHT:
USS Los Angeles (ZR-3) Entering Hangar, 1924
The USS *Los Angeles* is shown entering its hangar at Lakehurst, New Jersey. Note how tiny the crowds of people are compared to the airship. *The Library of Congress Prints & Photographs Division.*

Z R 3 Entering Hangar First Time
Naval Air Station   Lakehurst, N.

Balloons at rest, 1919
Considerably smaller than rigid
Zeppelins (but still quite large),
were the non-rigid blimps. Six are
shown at rest in Arcadia, California.
*The Library of Congress Prints &
Photographs Division.*

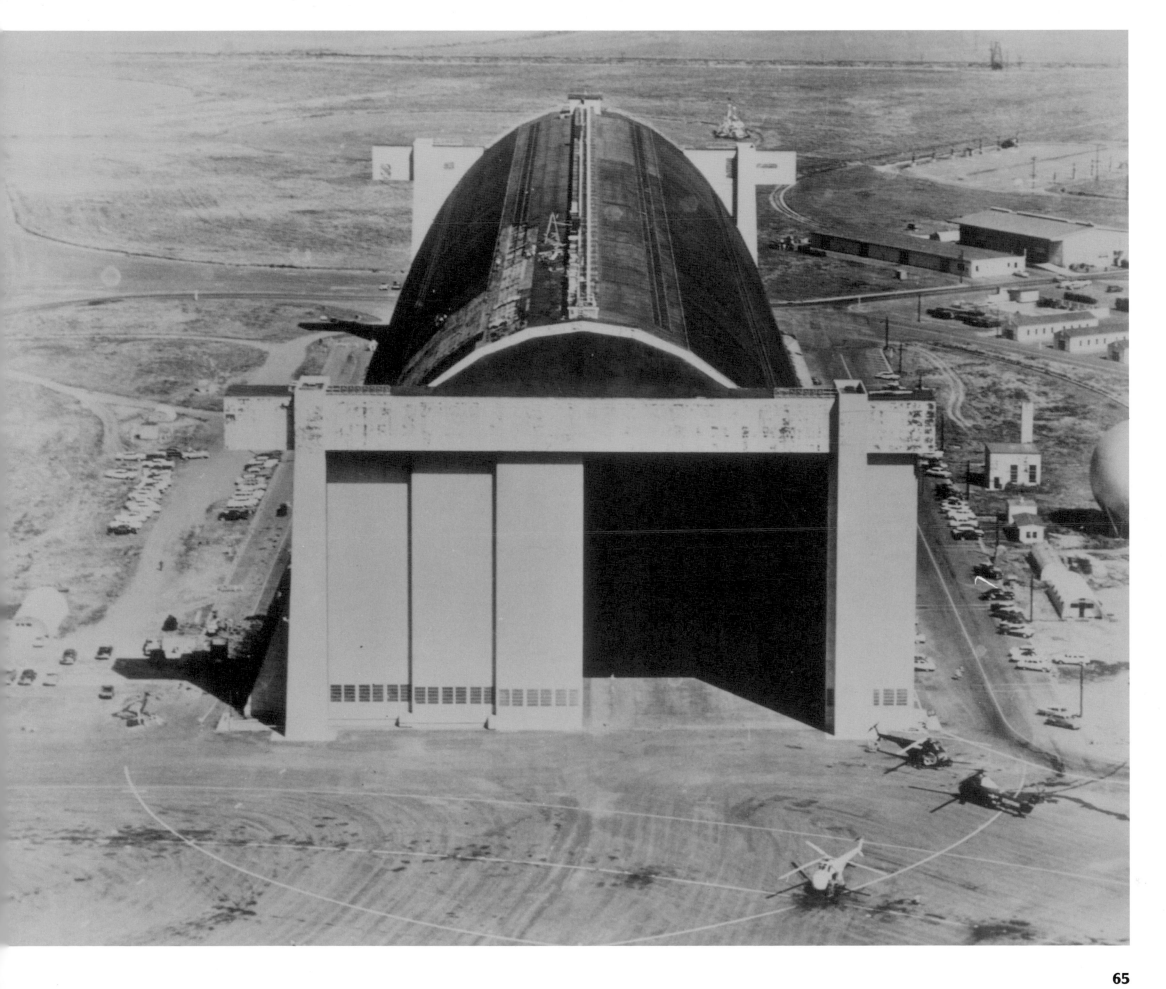

LEFT:
THE CALIFORNIA ARROW, 1904
Aeronaut A. Roy Knabenshue successfully demonstrates the maneuverability of T.C. Baldwin's 52ft *California Arrow* at the 1904 Louisiana Purchase Fair in St. Louis. *The Library of Congress Prints & Photographs Division.*

"To propel a dirigible balloon through the air is like pushing a candle through a brick wall."

ALBERTO SANTOS-DUMONT, **regarding Count Zeppelin's airship**

BELOW:
WELLMAN AIRSHIP, AMERICA, 1910
The *America* was a non-rigid airship built for Walter Wellman's attempt at polar flight. In 1909 he decided to try a transatlantic crossing and had to abandon the ship, seen here for the last time from the *Trent*. *The Library of Congress Prints & Photographs Division.*

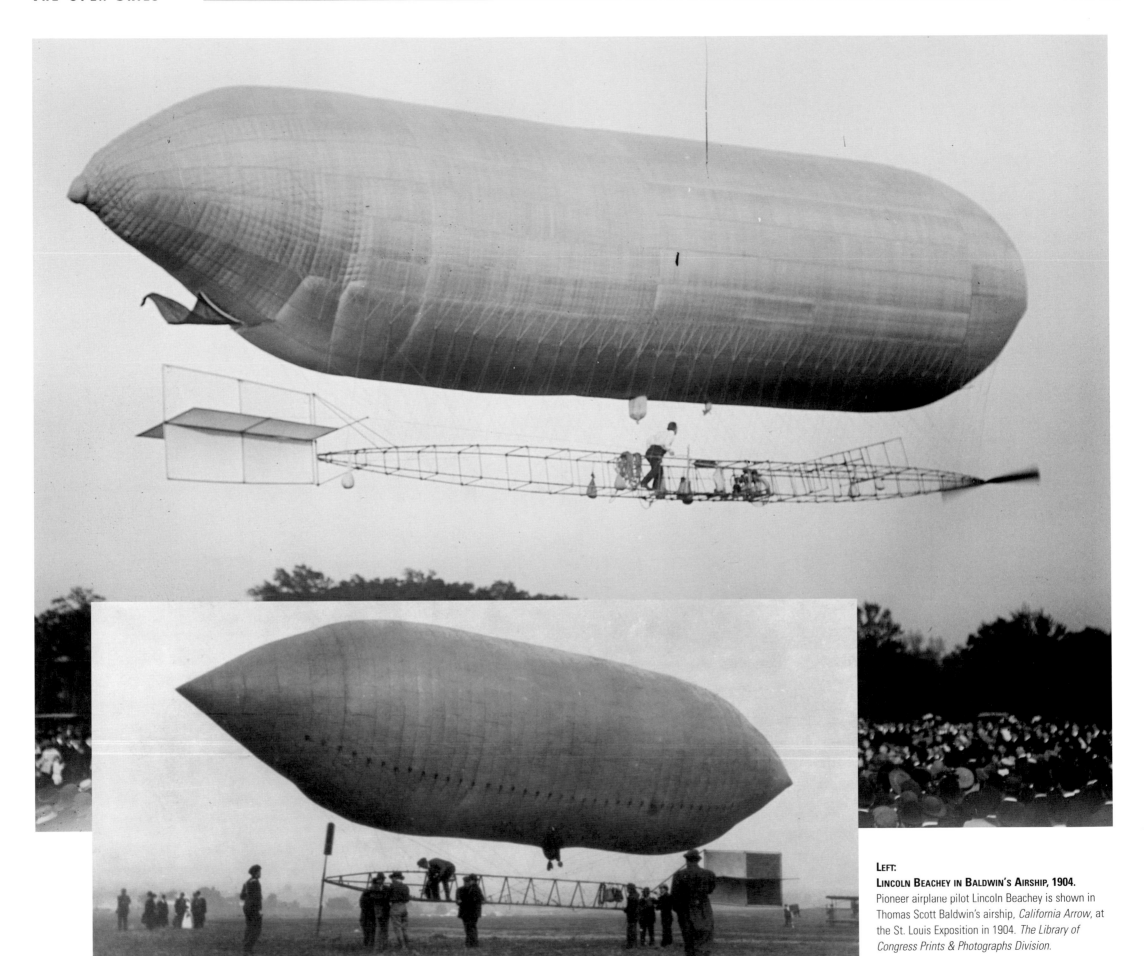

LEFT:
LINCOLN BEACHEY IN BALDWIN'S AIRSHIP, 1904.
Pioneer airplane pilot Lincoln Beachey is shown in Thomas Scott Baldwin's airship, *California Arrow*, at the St. Louis Exposition in 1904. *The Library of Congress Prints & Photographs Division*.

ABOVE LEFT AND ABOVE:
THOMAS BALDWIN.
Captain Thomas Baldwin (1860–1923) was a pioneer balloonist who developed the famous motorized balloon *California Arrow* which made the first controlled circular flight in America in St. Louis, August 1904. The U.S. Army Signal Corps was immediately interested in the craft's possibilities and paid Baldwin $10,000 to devise a dirigible suitable for controlled and sustained navigation. The resultant craft was SC-1 (Signal Corps 1) and was powered by a Curtiss engine. Baldwin went on to successfully design airplanes. These two pictures show a Baldwin balloon flying and on the ground in May 1909. *The Library of Congress Prints & Photographs Division.*

U.S.S. AKRON OVER MANHATTAN, 1931-33
USS *Akron* (ZRS-4), one of three German airships received as World World I reparations, is shown flying over the southern end of Manhattan Island, New York City.
U.S. Naval Historical Center.

U.S. NAVY DIRIGIBLE AND CREW
Dirigibles performed with some success in World War I and postwar development saw transatlantic services in operation. It would take the dramatic *Hindenburg* disaster to show up the dangers and end major commericial airship opertaions.
The Library of Congress Prints & Photographs Division.

"The R-101 is as safe as a house, except for the millionth chance."

LORD THOMSON, British Secretary of State for Air, **shortly**
before boarding the doomed airship headed to India on its first real proving flight, October 4, 1930. The day before he had made his will.

LEFT:
VANIMAN AIRSHIP AKRON BEFORE SAILING, 1911
Melvin Vaniman, who built the *Akron* (not to be confused with the Naval airship *Akron* of the 1930s), served aboard the *America*, which disappeared; he then perished in his *Akron* on July 2, 1912. *The Library of Congress Prints & Photographs Division.*

RIGHT:
"GIVE 'ER THE GUN." 1917
Blimps and airships are inclluded on this World War I recruitiung poster.. *The Library of Congress Prints & Photographs Division.*

RIGHT:
U.S. ARMY BLIMPS, C. 1920S
Two U.S. Army blimps, TC-5 and TC-9, from Langley Field, Virginia., pass over the Washington Monument during a practice flight. *The Library of Congress Prints & Photographs Division.*

FAR LEFT:
ZEPPELIN PASSENGER CABIN,
CA. 1928
A passenger cabin aboard the airship *Graf Zeppelin*, LZ-127 shows why airship travel was considered the height of luxury during the 1930s. *The Wisconsin Historical Society Historical Images.*

CENTER LEFT:
GRAF ZEPPELIN, ROUND-THE-WORLD
FLIGHT, 1929
The airship *Graf Zeppelin* is shown at rest at Los Angeles August 26, 1929, during its "Round-the-World" tour, starting and ending at Lakehurst, New Jersey. *The National Archives.*

LEFT:
BRITISH AIRSHIP R-101, 1930
The ill-fated British *R-101*, which crashed on its maiden flight on October 5, 1930 (effectively ending the British use of rigid airships), is pictured dropping water ballast. *The National Archives.*

THE AIRPORT

The earliest passenger airports were little more than hangars in grassy fields. Aircraft were not yet heavy enough to require either tarmac or concrete surfaces for landing, and grass on runways was cut two or three times per season. As aircraft grew larger and carried more passengers, the need for larger airports, better organization, more solid landing surfaces, and comfortable surroundings became clear, and the control tower became the most important part of an airport, helping to track and control rapidly increasing air traffic. Airports in some locations became works of art, and during the 1930s, the Works Progress Administration projects built a number of attractive airports with interesting designs.

Increased air traffic—originally tracked with small models on maps—was also the cause of many airport redesigns, with multiple, attached terminals eventually becoming the norm.

Despite these improvements in metropolitan areas, small rural airports still remained rather crude well into the 1960s, with no jet service available and grass runways as the norm. In some cases aircraft had to be towed to the terminal from a grassy field by farm tractors.

RIGHT:
NEWARK AIRPORT, UNDATED
As airports increased in size and serviced more passengers, the need for efficient parking grew as well, with multiple lots added to larger airports. *The Library of Congress Prints & Photographs Division.*

BELOW RIGHT:
LAGUARDIA AIRPORT, UNDATED
The old LaGuardia (New York) airport, built in 1940, featured a much more compact design than was required within a few years. Note the flying fish frieze near the top of the building. *The Library of Congress Prints & Photographs Division.*

FAR RIGHT:
MIAMI AIRPORT, C. 1934
An aerial view of Miami Airport shows the rear and side of the terminal, with docks extending outward for flying boats. *The Library of Congress Prints & Photographs Division.*

LEFT:

MIAMI AIRPORT, MAIN ELEVATION, C. 1934

The main entrance of the Miami Airport shows how close vehicles parked, in this case just yards from the door in a circle drive and next to the building. *The Library of Congress Prints & Photographs Division.*

ABOVE:

MIAMI AIRPORT, INTERIOR, C. 1934

A spacious interior shows passengers examining a gigantic set-in globe, with ticket counters in the background. Note the "time flies" clock motif. *The Library of Congress Prints & Photographs Division.*

RIGHT:

AIR TRAFFIC CONTROL, 1937
The earliest form of air traffic control involved moving plane models across maps as shown here in Cleveland's Air Traffic tower in 1937. *The Library of Congress Prints & Photographs Division.*

BELOW:

HANGAR ROW, CLEVELAND, 1937
"Hangar Row," as it was known, was the long, straight row of hangars for each of the different airlines, adjacent to runways. *The Library of Congress Prints & Photographs Division.*

LEFT:
BOARDING GATES, CLEVELAND, OHIO, 1937
This exterior view of the Cleveland Municipal Airport shows the open-style boarding gates near the main building, a system that became confusing with increased traffic. *The Library of Congress Prints & Photographs Division.*

BELOW:
BOARDING AREA, CLEVELAND, OHIO, 1937
Once passengers made it out to the tarmac from the terminal, they were confronted with airplanes parked in a long row. *The Library of Congress Prints & Photographs Division.*

FAR LEFT:
EASTERN DC-3, C. 1940S
N88813 had a varied life, serving with the USAAF until on December 19, 1946 when it went to Eastern Airlines Inc. It was involved in a midair incident with another DC-3 near Aberdeen, Md, but both aircraft were able to land safely. *National Archives.*

LEFT:
PURCHASING A TICKET, 1941
As a prelude to long waits and packed lines, here a passenger is seemingly leisurely purchasing his ticket in 1941 in Washington, D.C. *The Library of Congress Prints & Photographs Division.*

LEFT:
WASHINGTON NATIONAL AIRPORT, C. 1930S
The old Washington National Airport featured packed dirt runways during the 1930s. A small bank of dirt was all that separated parking from taxiing planes. *The Library of Congress Prints & Photographs Division.*

LEFT:
LONG-DISTANCE TRAVEL
The 1940s saw the start of international air travel as we know it today. TWA began crossing the Atlantic in 1946 using Lockheed Constellations. This "Connie" is at Paris's Orly airport.. *National Archives.*

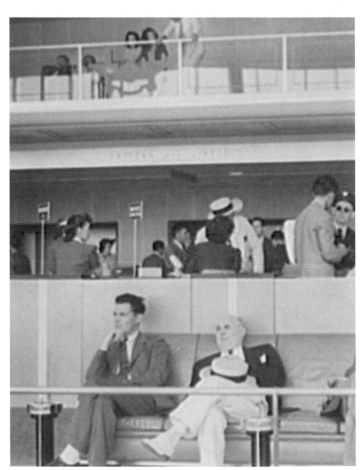

LEFT:

VIEWS OF MUNICIPAL AIRPORT, WASHINGTON, D.C., 1941

Both indoor and outdoor observation decks can be seen in these 1941 images. Such decks have always been popular spots with travelers or families. *The Library of Congress Prints & Photographs Division.*

ABOVE:

AIRPORT ADMINISTRATION BUILDING, 1939

This 1939 image shows the Airport Administration Building Fort Worth, Texas: it illustrates the combined aspects of form, function, and beauty. *The Library of Congress Prints & Photographs Division.*

FAR LEFT:
NORTH CENTRAL PLANE,
NOVEMBER 25, 1966
A North Central airplane sits at Austin Straubel Airport in Green Bay, Wisconsin. Green Bay, like many smaller municipal airports, was an important "mini-hub" for the numerous air services then in operation. *The Wisconsin Historical Society Historical Images.*

LEFT:
WASHINGTON NATIONAL AIRPORT,
AUGUST 1962
Eastern Airlines Lockheed Super Constellations at Washington National Airport in August 1962. These aircraft were used in the ground-breaking Washington–New York–Boston shuttle services (no booking, guaranteed seat), which had commenced the previous year. *The National Archives.*

LEFT:
LAGUARDIA AIRPORT, JUNE 29, 1949
Rows of benches and a long railed walkway make up the observation deck at LaGuardia Airport. The boarding area is just below the deck. *The National Archives.*

91

ABOVE:
MARINE AIR TERMINAL INTERIOR,
NEW YORK, 1940
The Marine Air Terminal in New York featured an extremely stylish and modernistic approach, complete with murals and terminal-in-the-round design. *The National Archives.*

RIGHT:
McCORMICK FARMALL CUB TRACTOR TOWING AIRPLANE, MAY 1949
Runways weren't always concrete or tarmac. An airport worker uses a McCormick Farmall Cub tractor to tow a small twin-engine airplane at a rural airport. *The Wisconsin Historical Society Historical Images.*

ATLANTA AIRPORT, C. 1930S
A Delta Airlines plane noses in to the Atlanta, Georgia, airport terminal, as a small crowd watches the event from the observation deck. *The National Archives.*

LEFT:
CHICAGO'S MIDWAY AIRPORT, C. 1950S
The stretched-out appearance of Chicago's Midway terminal illustrates how inefficient such design is by today's standards that have to serve much higher air traffic. *The National Archives.*

LOGAN AIRPORT, JUNE 1959
American Airlines *Lake Superior* sits on the tarmac at Logan Airport, Boston, awaiting boarding. Other aircraft can be seen in the background. *Photo courtesy Richard Leonhardt, photographer.*

BIRDS IN FLIGHT

For many years a favorite trip for many families was to go the airport to visit the facility's observation deck. From there children could see aircraft take off, land, and taxi. It also was a great way to get to know the different aircraft types and be able to identify them from a distance. To that end, decks of playing cards known as "spotter decks" were circulated widely through the military and civilian channels. Each card featured a bottom view, profile, and head-on silhouette of various aircraft that could be "spotted" and identified, becoming a popular game of its own.

Although most of these decks were military in origin (and developed for national security), they were fun and were helpful in recognizing civilian aircraft—either for the civilian equivalent of military planes or for military aircraft converted for commercial use. Short trips to smaller, municipal airports created the opportunity to spot small, private aircraft, such as Pipers, Cessnas, Beechcraft, and others.

The sight of an aircraft in flight always seems to stir the imagination about traveling in most everyone, even if there is no immediate possibility of going anywhere. It's not unusual to wonder where an airplane is coming from, where it's going, and who it's carrying when it flies high overhead and off into the distance.

| 1880 | 1885 | 1890 | 1895 | 1900 | 1903 | 1905 | 1908 | 1910 |

First glider flight. John J. Montgomery began a series of glider flights at Otay Mesa, California (March 17, 1883).

First parachute jump. Thomas E. Baldwin jumps from a balloon at San Francisco, CA (January 30, 1887).

The Wright Brothers build first glider with independent controls for wings. These are the forerunners of ailerons, which are used to control rolling and banking (1899).

The second and last trial of the Samuel Langley airplane, piloted by Charles Manly, was wrecked in launching from a houseboat on the Potomac River in Washington, D.C. (December 8, 1903).

The Wright Flyer becomes the first powered heavier-than-air craft to fly on December 17, 1903 (Orville piloted first flight). The craft flies 120 feet in 12 seconds.

A complete flight circle is made by a powered airplane (September 20, 1904) by Wilbur Wright.

The first fully controllable and maneuverable flight is made at Dayton, Ohio (June 23, 1905).

The first Aero Exhibition is held in New York City in conjunction with an annual auto show (January 1906).

First passenger. Wilbur Wright took Charles Furnas, an employee, on a flight check (May 14, 1908). The Wrights did not fly together until May 25, 1910.

Glenn H. Curtiss flies more than a mile at a public demonstration at Hammondsport New York (July 4, 1908). His plane is equipped with wingtip ailerons, which brings a warning from the Wrights about patent infringement.

Wilbur Wright gives first public demonstration of flight in LeMans, France (August 8, 1908).

First pilot license issued 1910. Glenn Cu receives license No. 1. Orville Wright rece No. 4 and Wilbur No. 5. Early licenses w assigned alphabetically.

First commercial flight school opens Montgomery, AL, operated by Orville W (March 19, 1910). The site later beca Maxwell AFB.

First city-to-city flight made. Glenn Cu flies from Albany, NY, to New York Cit distance of about 150 miles (May 29,

First woman solo pilots a powered air Blanche Stuart Scott is given cred (September 2, 1910), although it is nc certain the flight (a few seconds) was intentional or caused by wind).

First U.S. president to fly. Theodore Roosevelt, (out of office) rode with Arc Hoxsey at a St. Louis flying meet (Octol 11, 1910).

The first all-aviation exhibition was th Boston Aero Show (February 16, 1910

This Page and Following:
C-87 Fort Worth, Texas

World War 2 changed the face of flying forever. By the end of the war, there were hundreds of surplus pilots, engineers, and aircraft that formed the basis of many a transport company. They had worked on the many thousands of transports that were needed to fly men and materiel around the globe—such as the aircraft from U.S. Air Transport Command that had been flown by civilian crews, many from U.S. civil airlines. These pictures from October 1942 show the test flight of a C-87 Liberator Express and other scenes from Consolidated Aircraft Corp.'s Fort Worth, Texas facility. The transport variant of the B-24 Liberator, the C-87 was nowhere near as successful as its bomber version and would be superseded by the Douglas C-54.

The Library of Congress Prints & Photographs Division.

1911   **1912**   **1914**   **1916**   **1918**   **1920**   **1922**   **1924**

The first municipal airport is established at Modesto, California, 1911

Harriet Quimby becomes first licensed female pilot (License No. 37), 1911.

The first commercial aircraft manufacturer (Burgess & Curtis Co.) is established (February 1, 1911) at Marblehead, MA., and receives authorization from the Wright Co.

The first authorized mail delivery by air was made February 17, 1911 (18 miles), flown by Fred Wiseman from Petaluma to Santa Rosa, CA.

Cal Rodgers makes the first transcontinental flight in his Vin Fiz Flyer (September 17- November 5, 1911), from Sheepshead Bay, NY, to Pasadena, CA (about 3,395 miles).

The first official air mail delivery was made September 15, 1911 (six miles), flown by Earl Ovington from Long Island to Mineola, NY.

First parachute jump is made from an airplane (March 1, 1912).

Wilbur Wright dies of typhoid (May 30, 1912).

The first passenger service is established when Benoist Aircraft Co. (based in St. Louis) provides local air service between St. Petersburg and Tampa, Florida (January 1, 1914).

Official Air Mail service begins between Washington, D.C., and New York City (May 15, 1918).

First transatlantic flight (May 16-31, 1919). Lt. Cmdr. Albert C. Read and pilot Lt. Walter Hinton (U.S. Navy) make the crossing (about 4,500 miles) in a Curtiss NC-4 from Long Island, New York, to Plymouth, England, via Newfoundland, the Azores, and Lisbon.

First transcontinental air mail service (February 22, 1921). The flight goes from Mineola, New York, to San Francisco, California, in a de Havilland DH-4M, in 23 hours, 23 minutes.

The first global flight is made (April 6-September 28, 1924). Four Douglas DWC World Cruisers started from Seattle, Washington. Only two planes completed journey.

The first non-stop transcontinental flight is made (May 2-3, 1923).

First controlled (horizontal) flight in a helicopter (June 16, 1922). A warsurplus Nieuport biplane fighter is modified with tilting tail rotor, and a short-span upper wing with helicopter blades at the tips.

First airline ticket agency, Aeromarine Airways of Cleveland, Ohio, is established (July).

rtiss
ives
ere

n
ght
e

rtiss
a
0).

ne.

t

h
er

e

1925   **1927**   **1929**   **1930**   **1933**   **1937**   **1940**   **1950**   **1960**   **1970**

Contract air mail service established (February 2, 1925). President Calvin Coolidge signed the Kelly Bill, authorizing contract air transport of U.S. mail by commercial air carriers that received subsidies for performing the service.

First autogiro flight made in Willow Grove, Pennsylvania (December 19, 1928).

The *Hindenburg* burns as it attempts to land in New Jersey (May 6, 1937).

The first commercial airliner to exceed the speed of sound is a Douglas DC-8-53, during a brief dive in April 1962.

First American turbojet engine, the Westinghouse X19A, is designed in March 1943.

Charles Lindbergh completes first solo non-stop flight across the Atlantic Ocean (May 21, 1927).

The *Graf Zeppelin* begins transatlantinc and round-the-world service in August 1929.

The first stewardesses become part of an experimental program through United Airlines (May 15, 1930).

British pilot Frank Whittle develops the first jet engine.

First presidential aircraft. In 1930 one U.S. Navy aircraft was officially assigned for executive use by Franklin D. Roosevelt, but it would be 10 more years before he flew in an airplane.

The durable Douglas DC-3 is introduced in 1936. It becomes the most successful workhorse aircraft.

Igor Sikorsky's VS-300 helicopter makes its first successful flight in May 1940.

Domestic jet passenger service is established December 10, 1958 with National Airlines route between New York City and Miami, FL.

The first commercial jet, the Comet, makes its first flight in July 1949.

Pan American Airways is founded with a mail route between Key West, Florida, and Havana, Cuba.

The first jet airplane, the Bell XP-59A (piloted by Robert Stanley), is flown at Muroc AFB CA (October 1, 1942).

The Boeing 747 jumbo jet makes its first flight (February 9, 1969).

"*The desire to fly is an idea
handed down to us by our
ancestors who . . . looked
enviously on the birds soaring
freely through space . . . on the
infinite highway of the air.*"
WILBUR WRIGHT

ABOVE:
**MISS LILLIAN BOYER, AERIAL
ACROBAT, JANUARY 21, 1922**
One of the very few female aerial
acrobats was Lillian Boyer, a
waitress who began climbing out on
wings of flying craft her second
time in the air. *The Library of
Congress Prints & Photographs
Division.*

RIGHT:
**LATHAM FLYING OVER THE GOLDEN
GATE, 1911**
An early aircraft is shown flying
over San Francisco's Golden Gate,
26 years before the now-famous
bridge was completed. *The Library
of Congress Prints & Photographs
Division.*

LEFT:
AIRPLANE, 1923
A man in a low-flying biplane prepares to drop something to another man below. The decorated mast of a ship and an exposition building appear in the background. *The Library of Congress Prints & Photographs Division.*

ABOVE:
OBSERVATION PLATFORM, WASHINGTON MUNICIPAL, 1941
Few places gave people a better view of the comings and goings, and landings and takeoffs of aircraft than observation platforms at airports. *The Library of Congress Prints & Photographs Division.*

"I think it is a pity to lose the romantic side of flying and simply to accept it as a common means of transport, although that end is what we have all ostensibly been striving to attain"

AMY JOHNSON, *Sky Roads of the World,* 1939

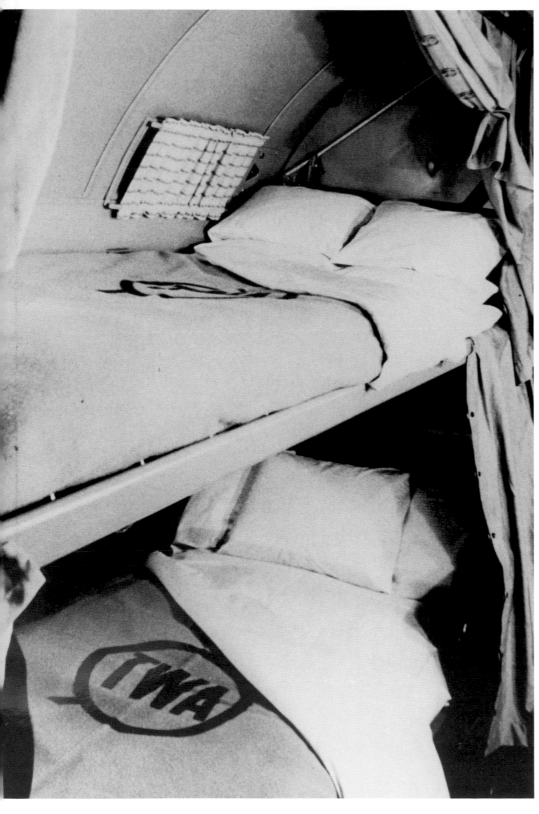

ABOVE:
TWA DST SLEEPER
In 1936 American Airlines started a coast to coast sleeper service using the 14-passenger Douglas DC-3 sleeper version—the DST. Other airlnes soon followed. *National Archives.*

ABOVE:
SEATTLE, 1940s
Boeing, based in Seattle, would become the postwar powerhouse of the aviation manufacturing world. But first it had to build WW2's best Flying Fortress. *National Archives.*

ABOVE:
NATIONAL AIR RACES, 1936
A large crowd watches planes go by at the 1936 National Air Races in Los Angeles, California. The races were held from 1920 to 1949. *Photo courtesy Steve Turechek.*

RIGHT:
DC–3, UNITED AIRLINES, 1939
A shiny, new Douglass DC–3 —one of the earlier models—makes its way through the clouds in 1939 as part of the United Airlines fleet. *The National Archives.*

LEFT:
BELL X–1 IN FLIGHT, C. 1947
The Bell X–1, a "flying bullet" was
the first to test flight at supersonic
speed. Three such jets (one piloted
by Chuck Yeager) were ordered for
testing purposes only. *The National
Archives.*

ABOVE:
SIKORSKY R4 HOVERFLY, C. 1940s
The Sikorsky R4 Hoverfly was the
world's first mass-produced
helicopter. It became quite popular
with the military shortly after the
"egg beater" first flew. *The
National Archives.*

THE PILOTS

The development of aviation, as we know it, could not have occurred as rapidly as it did or in any significant fashion without the hard work and daring exploits of the pilots: those brave, adventurous, bold, and sometimes stupid men (and a few women) who loved speed, the sensation of flight, and adventure.

Certainly the earliest U.S. pilots, including the Wright Brothers, Cal Rodgers, Lincoln Beachey, Harriet Quimby, Earle Ovington, and others, did much to set new records and establish and develop air travel. The end of World War I, however, brought a whole new breed of pilot to the forefront. These men, who learned to fly in the military and became World War I flying aces, were fearless. Although few lived to a ripe old age (most dying in various air mishaps), upon returning from the war they became the earliest commercial, airmail, and stunt flyers, as well as wing walkers and barnstormers.

Although the most well-known American pilots of the first few decades of flight are Charles Lindbergh and Amelia Earhart, many others were vital to the introduction and development of air travel, including Samuel Langley, Octave Chanute, Lawrence and Elmer Sperry, Igor Sikorsky, and others. Later pilots, including Chuck Yeager, captured the hearts and imaginations of millions of Americans and others all over the world with their accomplishments. Even modern-day pilots continue to captivate children all over the world, particularly when they present them with wing pins.

"Racing planes didn't necessarily require courage, but it did demand a certain amount of foolhardiness and a total disregard of one's skin. . . . I would be flying now, but there's precious little demand for an elderly lady air racer."

MARY HAIZLIP, Pioneer air racer

LEFT:
ROSCOE TURNER, 1936
Turner, three-time Thompson Trophy winner who set a new transcontinental speed record in 1930 (12h 33min), shown with parachute mounted on his back, climbs into his racer. *Photo courtesy Steve Turechek.*

LEFT:

JIMMY DOOLITTLE, 1931

Jimmy Doolittle, who would become famous for his actions in World War II, was a well-regarded racing pilot during the 1930s. He's shown here with his Laird Super Solution Racer. *Photo courtesy Steve Turechek.*

BELOW:

ROSCOE TURNER, 1936

Roscoe Turner, shown here with the Wedell Williams 44 Racer the year he won the Bendix Trophy, was one of the most accomplished of all early air racers. *Photo courtesy Steve Turechek.*

ABOVE:
LEE GELBACH, 1932
Lee Gelbach, a Bendix Trophy winner, is shown sitting on his Gee Bee R-2 Racer during the 1932 National Air Races in Cleveland, Ohio. *Photo courtesy Steve Turechek.*

ABOVE:
LILLIAN BOYER, JANUARY 21, 1922
Lillian Boyer, shown standing next to her plane, was an aerial acrobat at a time the field was populated almost entirely by World War I veterans. *The Library of Congress Prints & Photographs Division.*

RIGHT:
LINCOLN BEACHEY, 1912
Although Lincoln Beachey began his career flying dirigibles, he became one of the most well-loved of all pioneer aviators. He died in 1915 while performing a stunt. *The Library of Congress Prints & Photographs Division.*

ABOVE:
BLANCHE STUART SCOTT, C. 1910
Blanche Stuart Scott, who began driving in Rochester, New York, at age 13, became the first woman to both cross the country in a car and, later, in a plane. *The Library of Congress Prints & Photographs Division.*

ABOVE:
CHARLES K. HAMILTON, 1910
Charles K. Hamilton made the first round-trip flight between New York and Philadelphia on June 13, 1910, the day this photo was taken. *The Library of Congress Prints & Photographs Division.*

ABOVE:
CAL RODGERS, 1911
After Cal Rodgers made his historic first trans-continental flight in 1911, he was draped with a flag and greeted with flowers in Pasadena, California. *The Library of Congress Prints & Photographs Division.*

ABOVE:
LAWRENCE SPERRY, MARCH 21, 1922
Sperry is shown in a plane he hoped would become the "Fliver (Model T) of the air." It could fly 100mph, land on roads, and park in small spaces. *The Library of Congress Prints & Photographs Division.*

Harold F. McConnick

BILL DOTTER WAVING FROM HIS INTERNATIONAL HARVESTER AIRPLANE, 1948.

Pilot Bill Dotter waves goodbye just before taking off in the *Harold F. McCormick*, an International Harvester corporate airplane. Early corporate planes were converted B-23 light bombers. *The Wisconsin Historical Society Historical Images.*

LEFT:
BEECHCRAFT, LATE 1940s

A Wisconsin Central Airlines pilot walks toward a twin-engine Beechcraft airplane parked on the runway at Truax Field in Wisconsin. *The Wisconsin Historical Society Historical Images.*

"*I believe the risks I take are justified by the sheer love of the life I lead.*"

CHARLES A. LINDBERGH

LEFT:
CHARLES LINDBERGH, C. 1923-28
Lindbergh is shown here, wearing helmet with goggles up, in the open cockpit of an airplane at Lambert Field in St. Louis, Missouri. *The Library of Congress Prints & Photographs Division.*

RIGHT:
AMELIA EARHART, C. 1937
Amelia Earhart today is nearly as well known for being a women's advocate as she was for being a pilot. She was the first woman to be awarded the distinguished Flying Cross. *The National Archives.*

FAR LEFT:
CHUCK YEAGER AND GLAMOROUS GLENNIS, 1946 OR 1947
"Chuck" Yeager, Gus Lundquist, and Jim stand next to the Bell XS–1 supersonic rocket research airplane *Glamorous Glennis*, named for Yeager's wife. *The Library of Congress Prints & Photographs Division.*

LEFT:
MARY FECHET, FEBRUARY 19, 1929
Miss Mary Fechet, daughter of James E. Fechet, Chief of the Air Corps, stands by an airplane, facing left, in what was likely a publicity photo. *The Library of Congress Prints & Photographs Division.*

THE FRIENDLY SKIES

"Fly The Friendly Skies"
UNITED AIRLINES ADVERTISING, 1966

ABOVE:
WISCONSIN CENTRAL DC-3 CABIN, C. 1952
To celebrate the addition of DC-3s to its fleet, North Central Airlines sponsored special promotional events, including this special flight for handicapped World War II veterans. Food was served by president and co-founder, Francis Higgins. *The Wisconsin Historical Society Historical Images.*

The earliest passenger flights were not known for comfort. Passenger aircraft, for the most part, during the early 1920s, still had open cockpits (where the pilot wore goggles and flying jackets) and passengers sat in drafty, unheated cabins and were jostled and shaken throughout their flights. Even by the mid-1920s, when the Ford Trimotor appeared (with seating for 13–17 people), passengers sat in somewhat rickety (and certainly non-fastened) wicker chairs, and pilots couldn't be expected to care for the creature comforts of passengers. Passenger comfort, however, soon became a priority second only to passenger safety.

The first stewardesses, or flight attendants as they are known today, were not only required to be friendly and serve the needs of travelers but they had to be nurses as well, to serve the unexpected health needs of passengers.

Among the earliest of the "fine flying" experiences were aboard "flying boats," those aircraft designed to be able to land on open water. Most of these, operated by Pan-American Airlines in the United States, offered spacious cabins and meals that rivaled those found in fine restaurants. Soon, most airlines were competing to be the best in passenger service, whether it was friendly stewardesses, comfort of cabins or fine-quality food.

PASSING THE TIME IN THE PASSENGER LOUNGE, C. 1930S
Passengers smoke, play games, and work on a jigsaw puzzle in the lounge of a Pan American Sikorsky S.40 Flying Boat, which operated out of Miami to South America. *The Wisconsin Historical Society Historical Images.*

RIGHT:

TWA BAR AND LOUNGE, C. **1940S**
A steward serves four passengers in the bar and lounge of a TWA all-sleeper, trans-Atlantic Ambassador flight. Such flights were designed for utmost comfort. *The Wisconsin Historical Society Historical Images.*

ABOVE:
AMERICAN AIRLINES PILOT BRIEFS PASSENGER, UNDATED
A pilot with American Airlines outlines the route to an interested passenger, while a stewardess looks on. *The National Archives.*

"I've got the greatest job in the world. Northwest sends me to New York ten times a month to have dinner. I've just got to take 187 people with me whenever I go."

COLIN SOUCY, Northwest Airlines Pilot

ABOVE:
U.S. CUSTOMS, C. 1930S
A group of passengers goes through a customs check as they stand near their Western Air Express aircraft, Alhambra, California. *The National Archives.*

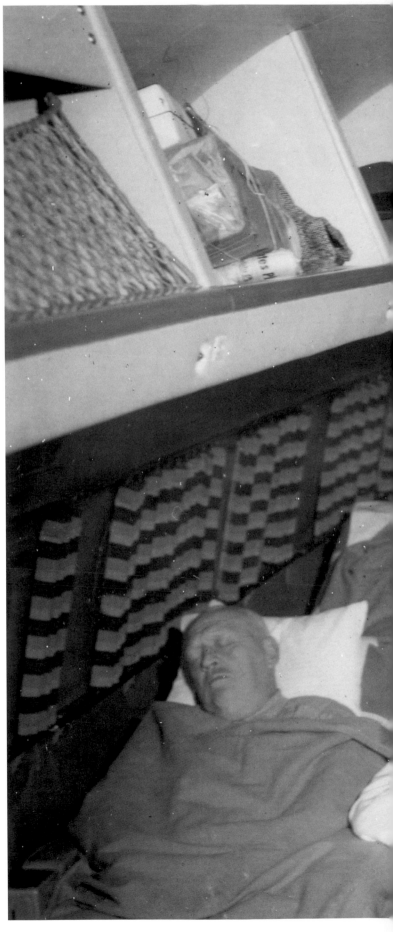

RIGHT:
TWA'S SLEEPING PASSENGERS, DECEMBER 1952
Passengers are shown napping aboard a TWA Constellation 803. By the early 1950s the Super Constellation represented the pinnacle of commercial airline travel, but these propeller-driven aircraft were soon replaced by jet engine aircraft. *The Wisconsin Historical Society Historical Images.*

RIGHT:

DINNER SERVICE, C. 1940S
A small group of travelers enjoys a full dinner, including plates and silverware, aboard a Douglas Sleeper Transport, a 14-berth sleeper version of the DC-3.
The National Archives.

FAR RIGHT:

CHECK IN, MADDOX TRANSCONTINENTAL AIR TRANSPORT, C. 1920S
Weighing passengers for load limit and weight distribution at check in was a necessary, if not slightly humiliating, part of early passenger service on small aircraft.
The National Archives.

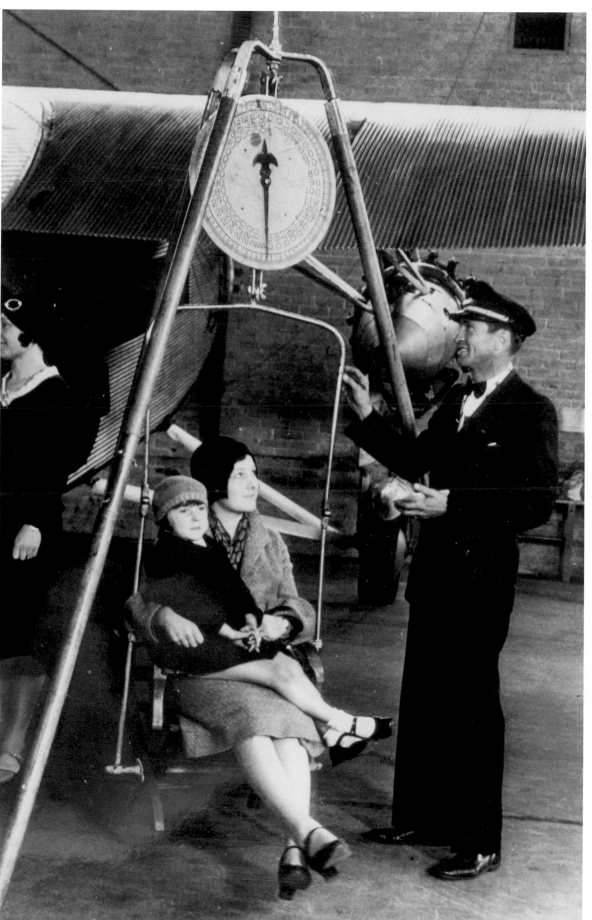

LEFT:
FIRST OFFICER SERVES TEA, C. 1930S
Before there were stewardesses
there was very limited on-board
service. In this case the first officer
serves tea to a woman passenger.
The National Archives.

ABOVE:
STEWARDESS, C. 1948.
A United Airlines stewardess in
uniform takes a moment to pose at
the base of the steps of a Douglas
DC-3. *Photo courtesy Bob Anderson.*

CURTISS CONDOR, C. 1934
Passengers and crew pose by a
Curtiss Condor airliner of Eastern
Air Transport, possibly a charter
flight. Condors pioneered the early
sleeper services. *The National
Archives.*

FOKKER TRI-MOTOR, C. 1920S
A group of passengers prepares to board an eight-twelve-passenger Fokker Tri-motor, which, along with the Ford Tri-motor, dominated the U.S. airline market during the 1920s. *The National Archives.*

LEFT:

TRANSCONTINENTAL PASSENGERS, 1941

Passengers aboard a transcontinental American airliner en route from Washington to Los Angeles, take time to look out the cabin window. John Collier, photographer. *The Library of Congress Prints & Photographs Division.*

BELOW:

NEW YORK'S MUNICIPAL AIRPORTS, 1937

A colorful poster showing a DC-3 and a Flying Boat promote New York's Municipal Airports as part of the Works Progress Administration Federal Art Project. *The Library of Congress Prints & Photographs Division.*

LEFT:
DISEMBARKING PASSENGERS, WASHINGTON, D.C., 1941
Passengers disembark from a rear entry on this Eastern Airlines "Silverliner" plane at Washington, D.C. Municipal Airport, while the ground crew works. Jack Delano, photographer. *The Library of Congress Prints & Photographs Division.*

BELOW LEFT:
AIRLINE HOSTESS, WASHINGTON, D.C., 1941
An airline hostess with Pennsylvania Central Airlines emerges from an airplane. She's wearing a full uniform, including hat, which was becoming popular at the time. Jack Delano, photographer. *The Library of Congress Prints & Photographs Division.*

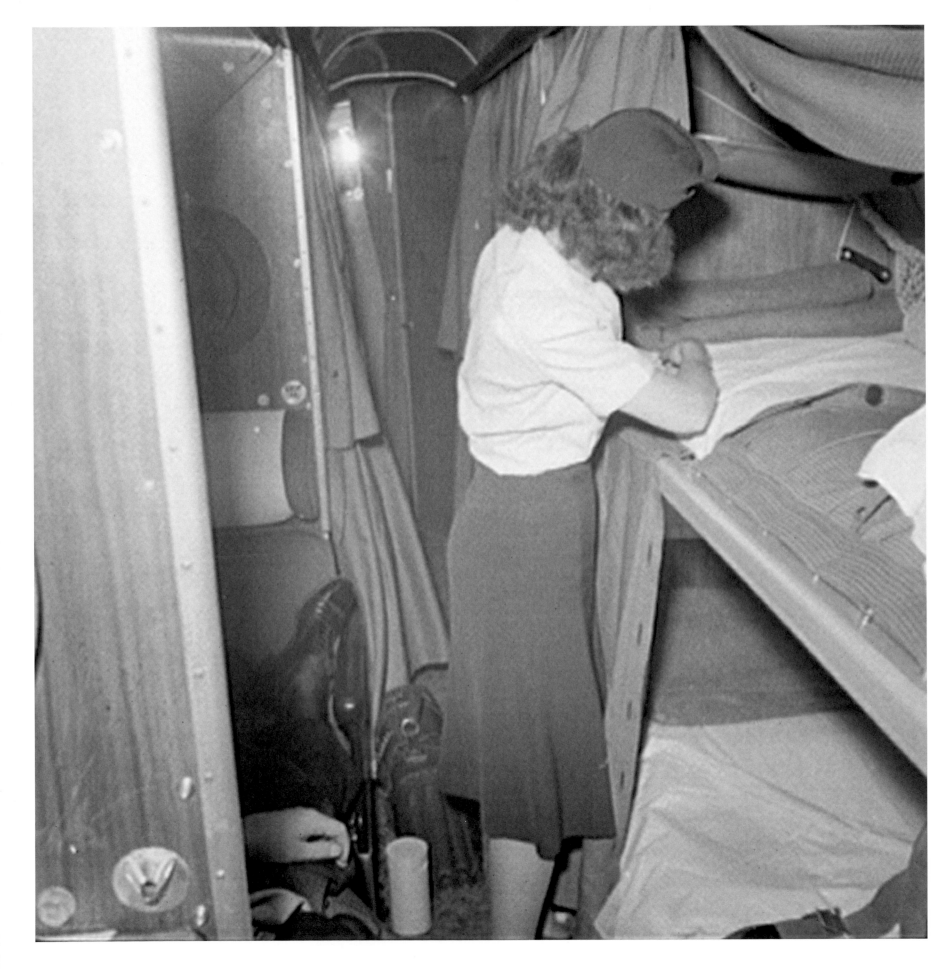

LEFT:
AMERICAN AIRLINER STEWARDESS, 1941
A stewardess makes up a bunk in a sleeping berth aboard an American airliner in San Francisco, California. A passenger is seen resting at left. John Collier, photographer. *The Library of Congress Prints & Photographs Division.*

FAR LEFT:
AIRLINE HOSTESS, WASHINGTON, D.C., 1941
As the role of stewardesses grew in commercial aviation, so did the glamor of being chosen as one. Stewardess schools became very popular during the 1940s and 1950s. Jack Delano, photographer. *The Library of Congress Prints & Photographs Division.*

BELOW:

AIRLINE STEWARDS, WASHINGTON, D.C., 1941

Even though stewardesses were rapidly taking over the role of passenger service and safety, there were still stewards working on the airlines during the early 1940s. *The Library of Congress Prints & Photographs Division.*

RIGHT:

INTERIOR, PEANUT ONE, 1976

Although most aircraft interiors were not as spacious as those of presidential jets, such as Jimmy Carter's *Peanut One*, jumbos provide many comforts. Thomas J. O'Halloran, photographer. *The Library of Congress Prints & Photographs Division.*

LATCH TABLE LEAVES CLOSED
FOR TAKE-OFF AND LANDING

ABOVE:
AIRLINE TICKET OFFICE, C. 1940S
In some ways airline ticket offices changed little for many years. Most, like this 1940s office, promoted deals with different airlines and had travel posters prominently displayed in the windows. *The Library of Congress Prints & Photographs Division.*

RIGHT:
IMPERIAL AIRWAYS OFFICE, C. 1940S
Many travel agencies and ticket offices "dress" their windows with airplane models and posters advertising exotic locations with excellent on-board service. *The Library of Congress Prints & Photographs Division.*

JUST FOR FUN

"Up in the air junior birdmen
Up in the air upside down
Up in the air junior birdmen
Keep your noses off the ground."

Thought to have originated as a light parody of the Army Air Corps song, "Into the air, Army Air Corps" by model airplane enthusiasts during the 1930s, the Junior Birdmen song became a favorite in camps all over the country. Swooping around camp with fingers bent around to create goggles was a source of air fun for kids for decades. And then there were the wingwalkers: those bold souls who did everything from gymnastics to pretending to play tennis while balancing on the wings of high-flying biplanes during the 1920s. They became heroes of sorts to kids and adults alike.

There's little question that air fever began soon after the invention of the airplane. Children pretended to be pilots, flying their imaginary planes around yards and playgrounds, or even in the house if mom didn't yell. Even various types of adult apparel of different periods reflected this national interest in flight. Model airplane clubs across America taught kids how to build airplanes while learning about flight and aerodynamics, and local businesses frequently found some sort of aerial tie-in to promotions. Flight continues to capture the attention and imagination of people of all ages.

RIGHT:
SAFETY LEAGUE MYSTERY SHIP, JULY 18, 1935
Airplanes captured the imagination of adults and children alike and became the center of many types of promotions, such as this B.F. Goodrich store venture. *The Wisconsin Historical Society Historical Images.*

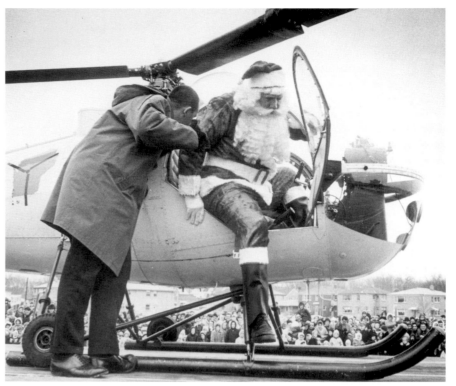

TOP:

FLYING SANTA, C. 1950S

Santa Claus emerges (with elfin help) from his special holiday helicopter at a shopping center somewhere in Wisconsin. *The Wisconsin Historical Society Historical Images.*

ABOVE:

PASSENGERS IN "COOLEY" AIRSHIP, C. 1910S

Wanting to cash in on the fever of flight, John F. Cooley built this grand airplane (81ft long and 42ft wide) that was supposed to travel more than 125mph. Construction was never completed. *The Library of Congress Prints & Photographs Division.*

TWINING ORNITHOPTER, C. 1909
Professor Twining's unsuccessful birdlike wing-driven ornithopter was criticized by a man who wrote, "No one would be foolish enough to build a motor boat driven by webbed feet or an automobile driven by legs like a horse's . . ."
The Library of Congress Prints & Photographs Division.

WRIGHT FLYER, 1903
But does the real thing look any better? The remarkable thing about the first aircraft is that today it looks as curious as madcap ideas such as Professor Twining's.
The Library of Congress Prints & Photographs Division.

ABOVE:
LILLIAN LORRAINE IN HER AIRSHIP,
C. 1909
Lillian Lorraine, an actress with the Ziegfeld Follies, "flew" above the audience in her "aeroplane" while singing a song in the 1909 Follies in a nod to the flight craze. *The Library of Congress Prints & Photographs Division.*

ABOVE RIGHT:
BLERIOT ENGINE, UNDATED
The engine and propeller of a Bleriot flyer shows the relative simplicity of the mechanics of early aircraft. *The Library of Congress Prints & Photographs Division.*

RIGHT:
"THINK IF THERE SHOULD BE AN ACCIDENT," C. 1910
This Frederick Coffay Yohn drawing shows a man pleading with a woman in a very early aircraft, from *Her Compelling Eyes*, a novel of the day. *The Library of Congress Prints & Photographs Division.*

FAR RIGHT:
CIRCUS PERFORMERS AND AIRPLANE, C. 1930
A giant and other circus performers pose near a Midwest Air Transport plane, part of a promotion to call attention to Orland Corben's Baby Ace monoplanes. *The Wisconsin Historical Society Historical Images.*

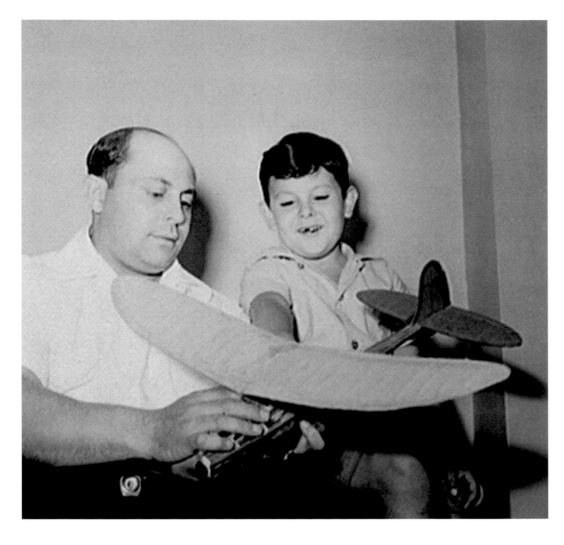

ABOVE:

MODEL AIRPLANE, BROOKLYN NEW YORK, 1942

Jimmy Caputo shows his father a model airplane at the Red Hook housing development in Brooklyn, New York. The hobby is credited with giving many young boys a positive focus. Arthur Rothstein, photographer. *The Library of Congress Prints & Photographs Division.*

RIGHT:

RODGERS, C. 1911

A pair of similarly dressed young girls—thought to be Cal Rodgers' daughters—sit in the cockpit of an early Wright Flyer. *The Library of Congress Prints & Photographs Division.*

CHRISTENING OF A SIKORSKY PLANE, MAY 8, 1925
Igor Sikorsky, who later invented the modern helicopter, opened the Sikorsky Aero Engineering Corp. in 1923. This was one of his early craft. *The Library of Congress Prints & Photographs Division.*

ABOVE:
THE GODDESS OF FLIGHT, 1921
A photographic allegorical mockup shows an attractive young woman in a dress pinned back to simulate flight. She holds a model airplane while posed on a globe. *The Library of Congress Prints & Photographs Division.*

MEN EXAMINING AIRPLANE ENGINE,
c. 1920s
Early aircraft were fairly simple to
repair, mechanically speaking. Here,
two men examine an airplane
engine on the farm. *The Library of*
Congress Prints & Photographs
Division.

RIGHT:
AERO MODELING, 1944
A young man runs along after his
model airplane, the largest entered
plane (with a wing span of 9 ½ ft) at
a meet at Modelhaven Airport, near
Baltimore, Maryland. *The Library of*
Congress Prints & Photographs
Division.

LEFT:

MODEL AIRPLANE, SAN ANTONIO, 1944

Orin Anderson poses behind his giant model plane at Kelly Field in San Antonio, Texas, where members of the Gas Model Club used to hold weekly flying events. *The Library of Congress Prints & Photographs Division.*

RIGHT:

INTERNATIONAL AVIATION MEET, 1912

The Third International Aviation Meet in 1912 (Oakland, California) produced several promotional postcards, such as this one, mentioning Blanche Stuart Scott's name. *Photo courtesy Nutmeg Auctions.*

ABOVE:
BIPLANE, C. 1920S
Early private aircraft were frequently used for a variety of purposes. This biplane, piloted by Gale Smiley, is painted with the logo of the Rose Lawn Poultry Farm. *Photo courtesy of the author.*

CENTER RIGHT:
TRAVEL AIR MYSTERY RACER, 1931
James G. Haizlip poses with a trophy in front of his Travel Air Mystery Racer at the 1931 National Air Races in Cleveland, Ohio. *Photo courtesy of Steve Turechek*

FAR RIGHT:
FLYING ACES MAGAZINE, MARCH 1936
As flight fever grew, so did publications to help hobbyists' enjoyment. *Flying Aces* magazine served to meet the needs of those seeking aerial "fiction, model building, and fact." *Photo courtesy of the author.*

PAN-AMERICAN AIR RACES PROGRAM, 1934
The Pan-American Air Races, held in New Orleans, Louisiana February 9–13, 1934, were just one of dozens of different air races held throughout the country during the 1930s, most emphasizing the fun of aviation. *Photo courtesy of Steve Turechek.*

LEFT:
LAIRD SUPER SOLUTION, 1931
Jimmy Doolittle piloted the Laird Super Solution at the 1931 National Air Races in Cleveland, Ohio, where he won the Bendix trophy. The plane is parked under the wing of a much larger craft. *Photo courtesy of Steve Turechek.*

BELOW:
NATIONAL AVIATION MEET, 1910
The first National Aviation Meet was held at the Indianapolis Motor Speedway, June 13–18, 1910, and attracted many types of aircraft, although some of these were likely pasted in to the photograph. *The Library of Congress Prints & Photographs Division.*

LEFT
PREPAREDNESS PARADE, 1916.
In an unusual sight, an airplane with its engine running sits on a White truck in a "Preparedness" parade in either New York City or Chicago. *The Library of Congress Prints & Photographs Division.*

FAR LEFT:
AVIATION THEMED HAT, LOS ANGELES, c. 1910
"Where did you get that hat?" a popular song near the turn of the century, applied to air-themed headgear such as this. *The Library of Congress Prints & Photographs Division.*

"No one would be foolish enough to build a motor boat driven by webbed feet or an automobile driven by legs like a

INDEX